THE COMPLETE GUIDE TO COMBAT CITY

JULIA SCHULZ-DORNBURG

jovis

Visit Combat City:

www.juliaschulzdornburg.com/combat-city

CONTENT

PREFACE

I began working on *The Complete Guide to Combat City* in 2018. The structure of the book was defined and the body of the work completed before Putin invaded the Ukraine on 24 February 2022. Britain has provided five-week military training courses to around 20,000 Ukrainians over the past year – many of those received their warfare preparation in Copehill Down, one of the mock-cities discussed in the book. The guide was already finished when the terrorist attack on Israel by Hamas took place on 7 October 2023. Most of the 360,000 Israeli reservists, involved in the massive Israeli retaliatory assault on Gaza, have received their urban warfare training in Baladia. The location of this simulated enemy town, also included in this guide, is a one-hour drive away from the Gaza Strip.

“As the world becomes more urban, we need to be prepared for cities to become battlefields.”

Modern War Institute, Urban Warfare Project, 2017

INTRODUCTION

The Complete Guide to Combat City looks at fictional enemy cities built by the military in Europe, the US and the Middle East to train for war. The current military doctrine "train as you fight" favours realistic hands-on training for its troops. Military doctrine considers the practise of urban warfare tactics in realistic urban environments to be an essential preparation for soldiers prior to deployment. Innumerable urban combat facilities have been built by contractors from the armed forces on army ground in the last eighty years. The military is the exclusive developer of these combat towns that have silently multiplied and spread throughout the western hemisphere. Unmarked on maps, and largely unnoticed by urban design, architecture and planning communities, these sites constitute a shadow global-city system. They are capsules of space designed to mimic the strategic environment of the city – now seen by the military as a critical arena for future wars.[1]

Cities, according to military academic research, are the future battleground. Russell Glenn argues in the preface of his research paper on urban warfare that the armed forces are ever more likely to fight in cities as the world becomes increasingly urbanised and the nature of battle methods change.[2] Conventional warfare is being replaced by asymmetric or irregular warfare, which is fast becoming the traditional means of waging a battle. The armed forces assume that most of these unconventional wars will be fought in cities. Reports from the Modern War Institute claim that insurgency, terrorism and resistance movements have already relocated their operational bases from the shelter of inaccessible territories to the protective anonymity of the city.

Military theorists consider cities, which are by their nature complex, unpredictable, messy, contradictory and ever changing, to be a natural stage for threats, terrorist attacks, demonstrations and other disruptive actions threatening order and control. Launching a military operation in a dense urban area, whether hostile or defensive, is challenging and complex. Conventional warfare tactics do not apply, troops must split into small autonomous fighting units that, in the best of cases, orchestrate a coordinated operation by improvising within the densely populated urban terrain. The prospect is daunting, and the potential casualties so high (urban warfare has no parallel, in scope or magnitude, in any other battle environment) that commanders want their armies to be well prepared.[3]

1 Stephen Graham, **Cities Under Siege: The New Military Urbanism,** p. 183, Verso, 2010.

2 Russell W. Glenn, **Combat in Hell, A Consideration of Constrained Urban Warfare,** Rand Monograph Report, 1996.

3 John Spencer, **The city is not neutral: Why urban warfare is so hard,** Modern War Institute, 04.03.2020.

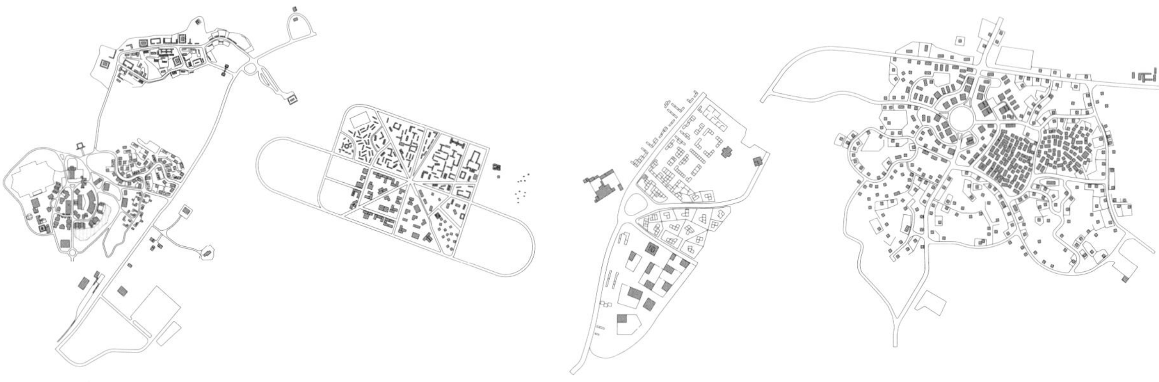

Urban warfare facilities, from left to right: Lejeune (US), Yodaville (US), Chinchilla (Spain), Baladia (Israel).

In this context, it is not surprising that urban combat training sites are in great demand. Many of these shadow cities are of considerable size. These elaborate, life-size replicas of enemy towns are designed to practise the art of war and to acclimatise the soldier with the aspect, rules and characteristics of the city that is to be invaded. A fortnight's immersion in one of these simulated combat sites has become standard training procedure prior to departing for war. As new armed conflicts arise, these mock-cities shed their skins and smoothly adapt their appearance to be reborn in the guise of the latest enemy.

Military restrictions and security measures make it difficult for the interested civilian to visit these sites in person. There is, however, extensive video coverage of these combat towns in action. Every training soldier is issued with a GoPro (a small mounted camera for close-up action shots), that records every move taken during the warfare training. The battle is filmed from as many angles as there are men on the field, creating a never-ending, shaky-handed stream of visual documentation about the city. Uncommon cityscapes strangely blur into endless sequences of running across a street amid explosions, climbing into windows and breaking down doors, shooting from the rooftops and holding hostages on the main square below the ever-present mosque. As exercises repeat and footage is added, the image of the city slowly emerges between billowing smoke and rifle fire.

The Complete Guide to Combat City is my second book on fictional cities. *Modern Ruins* (Ambit, 2012) surveyed unfinished vacation cities (casualties of the financial crisis and the bursting of the real estate bubble in 2008) and analysed the dreams, promises and fall-backs that led to the premature ruin of these wholesale paradises on Earth. *The Complete Guide to Combat City* looks at fictional enemy cities built by the military to train for war. Paradise and hell, swimming pools and machine-gun fire are antagonistic; but both, wellness and war, unfold in cities that are designed and built to simulate other, often faraway places.

The counterfeit architecture of speculative leisure enclaves uses the strategy of deception to bolster profits. The property market embellishes and masks reality, but it does not make it any less real. The artful stage-management of deception in combat cities on the other hand, produces real symptoms and hyperreal effects among the troops that begin to break

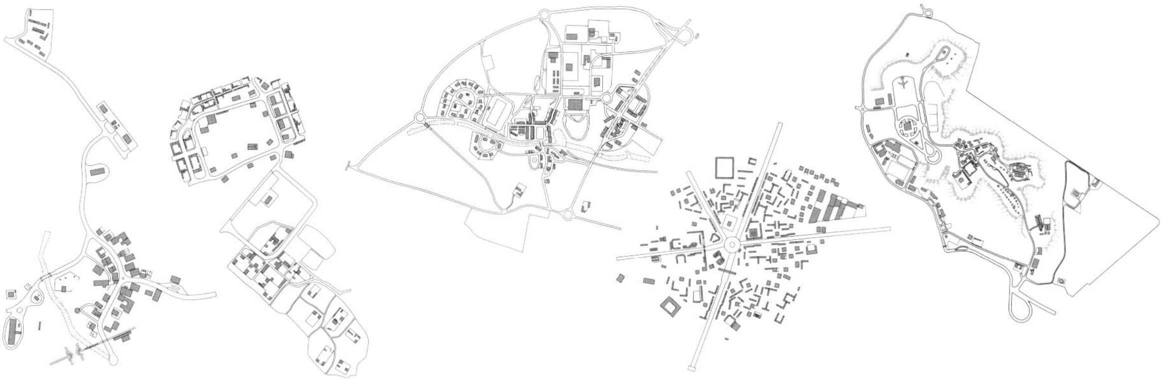

Urban warfare facilities, from left to right: Hohenfels (Germany), Eastmere (UK), Jeoffrécourt (France), Medina Wasl (US), KASOTC (Jordan).

down the differences between the simulated and the real. Notions of true and false, genuine and fake blur into a continuous vivid cityscape of displaced and reimagined urban scenarios populated by the "other".

If fake cities, fictitious enemies and staged combat can be experienced as genuine, is there any need to differentiate between authentic and simulated environments when analysing them? Does it actually matter? Many first-hand accounts from soldiers confirm the collapse in perceptual and cognitive distance in simulated cities during combat training. People, streets and buildings in these towns may not be authentic but they are definitely real, most of them at least. Real enough to stage terrifying urban combat on a convincing scale. Fake enough to be unique in its use, form and function. This publication embraces all pertinent cities' features, be they fictional or real, and presents them, commented, illustrated and classified as a city guide.

Are encyclopaedic templates for city guides (i.e. history, governance, geography, demography, economy, culture, religion and infrastructure) useful when it comes to describing urban simulations? Does it make them sound more real? Valid? Genuine? Is the fictional aspect a limitation or an asset for this kind of analysis? The intriguing question of whether simulated cities have the capacity to grow beyond their representational purpose, and constitute a viable town in their own right despite their fictional character, is one of the key issues this urban study aims to reveal. This city handbook will put the power of simulation to test and explore if the fake city can resist or even surpass the comparison with its mirror image. This illustrated publication provides a unique opportunity to tune out machine-gun fire and explosions and focus on the dwellers, the history, the urban culture and building style of these simulated city fragments.

This guide analyses the fundamental aspects of military mock-cities in an accumulative rather than a comparative fashion. The reasons are manifold. Cities are complex, living organisms with countless overlapping systems, connections, interests and cross purposes. Size and density are fundamental for the urban character of a settlement. Mock-cities are neither big nor very complex. They are purpose-built urban fragments that represent a larger whole, vignettes of a potentially more extensive, denser, and farther reaching city.

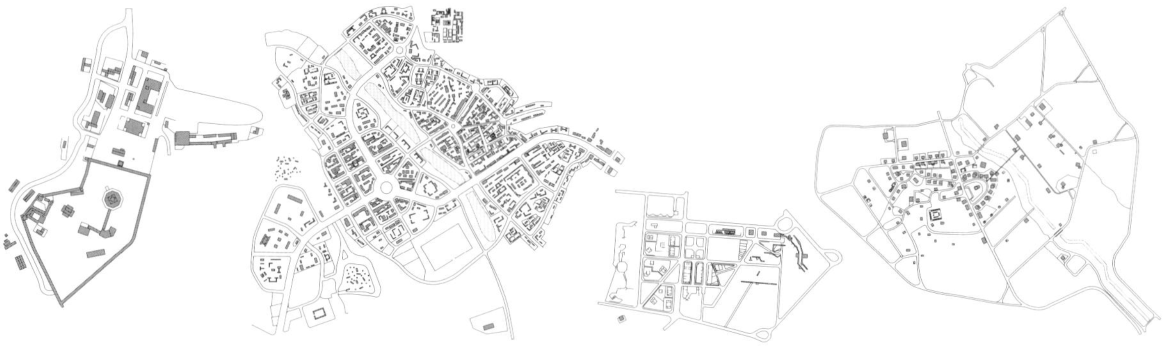

Urban warfare facilities, from left to right: Anaconda (US), Wadi al-Sahara (US), CTZUB (France), Marnehuizen (The Netherlands).

The image, layout and workings of a city cannot be extrapolated from a single representative sample, nor can this sample be its mere extension. A simple increase of the fragment in size would result in a homogeneous building pattern closer to a suburban sprawl than an urban fabric. An accumulative rather than extrapolative comparison of these township fragments will avoid the limited scope of the city samples and generate, by their addition, the appropriate size and complexity of a township without losing the specific qualities and characteristics of its constitutional elements. Embedding a variety of the different types of mock-cities as neighbourhoods into a greater city plan will produce a composite urban fabric and create a plausible city plan.

But there is more to a city than urban fabric. History and evolution also play an essential role in the forming of its character and spirit. Time foments changes and adaptions that will validate the cities' vitality and capacity to function. Combat towns have a short history, most of them are less than twenty years old. Nearly all of them are built from scratch and have had little time to develop beyond their initial scope. The vitality of these shadow cities will benefit from an integral analysis with the proposed urban mosaic of neighbourhoods. The pooling of the individual timelines enriches the urban chronicle and helps to reveal the correlation between cityscape and conflict over time.

The Complete Guide to Combat City reconstructs the physical aspect and daily workings of these urban combat centres from video footage, satellite images, military photographs, army supplier's catalogues as well as written information from military, academic and media sources. A selection of 17 existing, fully functioning urban combat centres located in the US, Europe and the Middle East make up the body of the work presented here. The cases are chosen for being architecturally elaborate examples of simulated cities in terms of size, complexity, relevance and sophistication. Every one of them is used for military pre-deployment training, the soldiers' last stepping stone before the actual battlefield.

A great number of shadow cities can be found throughout the world. However, military needs and budgets for simulated training cities vary greatly (hence the dominance of American sites) and not all of them are well documented. The research of Russian and Chinese urban combat centres, for instance, due to translation difficulties and digital access

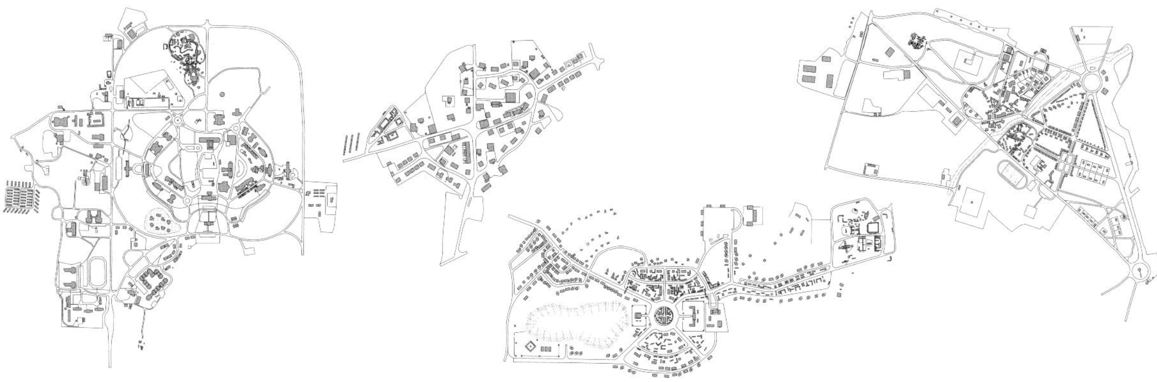

Urban warfare facilities, from left to right: Muscatatuck (US), Copehill Down (UK), Medina Jabal, (US), Schnöggersburg (Germany).

problems, does not yield sufficient information to confirm enigmatic satellite images and build a solid case. Others seemed irrelevant. The lack of academic sources or other sort of official information has required the use of additional, less formal documentation in some of the selected cases to complete the picture. The collection of simulated enemy cities presented in this publication, however incomplete, facilitates the detailed study of urban combat centres and ratifies the large scale construction of these "imaginative geographies" throughout homeland territory.[4]

The fictional removal of the geographic distance between them bonds the urban fragments into one large city with seventeen different districts. The poetic license of annulling the relative distance between them facilitates the analysis of fundamental aspects of the mock-cities and helps to unravel the urban complexities of the combat town. All numbers and figures, geographical conditions, orientation and size are taken from above mentioned sources and remain unaltered. *The Complete Guide to Combat City* looks at the specifics of the town, its people, language, culture, food and economics and describes it as what it presents itself to be: a city.

4 Imaginative geographies are self-constructions of the West that underwrite and animate its constructions of the other. See Edward W. Said, **Orientalism,** *Pantheon Books, 1978; Fernando Coronil,* **Beyond Occidentalism,** *in Cultural Anthropology 11, Vol. 1, pages 51–87, February 1996.*

HISTORY

The first chapter presents the nonagenarian history of Combat City and looks at how military conflicts have shaped the city. The construction of each of the 17 districts responds to a specific war. Each enemy has shaped the image of the city, leaving a distinct mark on the urban fabric and its buildings.

We begin with the first district, Hohenfels, which was inaugurated in 1938 to train German troops during the Second World War. Four years later, British soldiers rehearsed the battle of Normandy in the simulated Nazi village of Eastmere. The Israeli Defence Forces prepared the Lebanese invasion in the Middle Eastern district of Baladia. Camp Lejeune was founded during the Cold War and built in European style. It was later upgraded to prepare US troops for the Afghan War. The British Army prepared for the Irish Troubles in the Bavarian style mock-village of Copehill Down, which opened in 1988. Two years later, the Yugoslav Wars prompted intense training in the Marnehuizen, the Dutch take on a suburban village. Yodaville, which opened for bombing in 1999, is made from cluster-bomb containers used in the Vietnam War. The invasion of Iraq in 2003 drove the construction of orientalised districts like Medina Wasl, Medina Jabal, Wadi al-Sahara and Anaconda to cater for pre-deployment training of the US forces. The small, roofless district of Chinchilla began training the Spanish Armed Forces in non-specific conflict training in North Africa and the MENA region in 2007. The Jordanian King inaugurated the international warfare Olympics in KASOTC the following year. The French Army of the Land have trained for all eventualities in the native looking Jeoffrécourt since 2011. The German Army began to move their tanks through the unfinished district of Schnöggersburg in 2018.

Most of Combat City's districts are built, paid for or used by members of the NATO alliance with shared military interests. Takeovers and co-ownership between the seventeen combat training sites are common. Most joint ventures are driven by economic and geopolitical reasons. Other, less formal partnerships, promote the shared use of the facilities – so as to benefit from the synergistic effects of collective training sessions. This chapter reveals ties and unsuspected correlations between these players and aims to chart their game on the worldwide combat playing field.

Muscatatuck
Yoda-ville
Anaconda
Medina Wasl
Chinchilla
Lejeune
Marnehuizen
Copehill Down
KASOTC
Baladia
Jeoffrécourt
CTZUB
Hohenfels
Wadi al-Sahara
Schnöggersburg
East-mere
Medina Jabal
54° N
31° N

Rural Beginnings

In a remote inland region in the northern hemisphere, between the latitudes of 31° and 54°, a small 19th century German village dedicated to cattle breeding and agriculture remained relatively unchanged until the mid-20th century. Its traditional buildings were rather large and elongated with steep pitched roofs, plastered façades and small symmetrically placed windows. The barren soil of its pastures, the notorious lack of water and its geographic isolation ensured hardship and poverty for the dwellers of the village, whose population had been dwindling steadily. Everyday life was uneventful until the area attracted military attention in 1938 when it reincarnated itself as Hohenfels.[1]

A little further to the north, hidden in the folds of the terrain and sheltered by trees, lay a larger, predominantly American village with the Indigenous name of Muscatatuck, the land of winding waters. A few years earlier, in 1920, the "Indiana Farm Colony for the Feeble Minded", opened.[2] The Muscatatuck Colony, a work farm and residential facility, housed up to 3,000 developmentally disabled men over the age of sixteen as well as the 2,000 employees who were there to take care of them. The secluded, self-contained mental institution had been built to resemble a college campus with large lawns, flower beds, trees and fountains. The asylum's yellow brick buildings, built in geometric art deco style, were arranged in an axial garden fashion.

There was no formal or informal exchange between the two farm communities at this time. The "feeble minded" kept to themselves and the Germans stayed clear from what they considered to be a suspicious community with strange ways and an incomprehensible language. Anyhow, life was tough everywhere and the labour-filled days too short to rouse interest or curiosity about the "other". Cattle had to be raised and fed, crops had to be driven in and land prepared for the next season.

It was not until the eve of the Second World War that the arduous rural routine of the two farming communities changed for ever. Europe was about to be plunged into a new world conflict. Germany was openly flouting the military restrictions of the Versailles Treaty. While the size of the standing army was to remain at the 100,000-man mark, a new group of conscripts equal to this size would now receive training every year. Across the summer of 1938 Adolf Hitler intensified the pressure on neighbouring Czechoslovakia. War appeared increasingly likely.

1 *GlobalSecurity.org*, ***Hohenfels Training Area. US Army Garrison – Hohenfels Germany***, *www.globalsecurity.org/military/facility/hohenfels.htm, n.d., last visit: 23.04.2018.*

2 *Stew Magnuson*, ***Indiana Psychiatric Institution transformed into Urban Training Ground***, *National Defense Magazine, June 2010.*

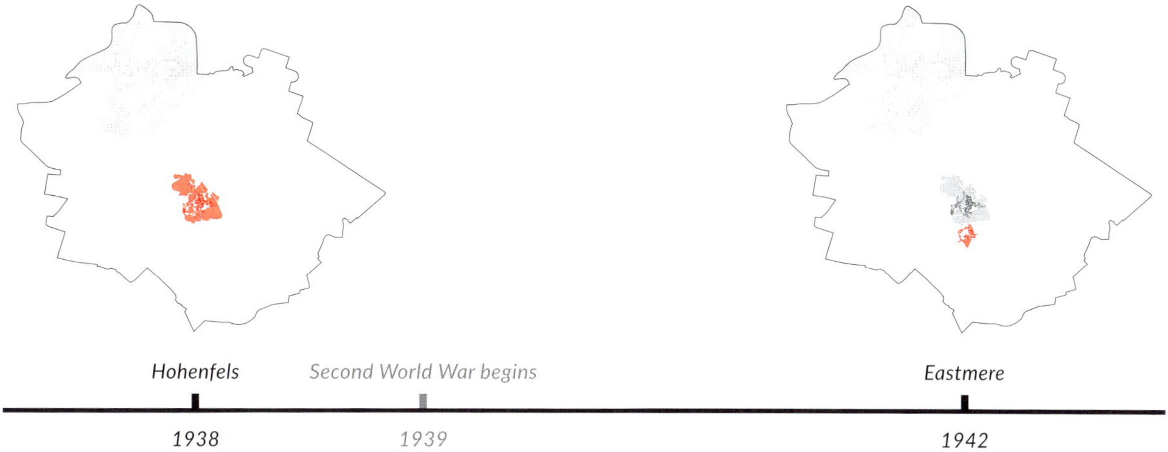

In preparation for the deadliest conflict in human history, the German Wehrmacht cleared the village of Hohenfels of its resident population and turned it into a training ground for its troops. Some 544 homesteads were converted into enemy quarters, tanks replaced cows and soldiers moved into what was to be the founding core of Combat City.[3] The outbreak of the Second World War prevented the execution of an ambitious construction plan for the training area. Administrative buildings for the command office, the army site administration and the Army Forestry Office never made it past the paper draft. None of the storage sheds for ammunition and field rations with a railway link, nor the hospital airfield or the anti-aircraft shooting range were completed. A 1,000-man barrack camp was the only structure to be finished on time. The troops moved in once the construction workers left, military training began in April 1939.[4]

On the other side of the Channel, the English were learning about the battle technique of lightning warfare or *Blitzkrieg* as the Germans called it. Many of the British recruits were civilians that had to learn how to function in the terrifying confusion of modern warfare. After the evacuation of Dunkirk, a large part of the conscript army had been cooped up in the United Kingdom with no prospect of sharpening its skills in action. Serious training for the upcoming D-Day was imperative.[5] From late 1940 onwards, the British began using live ammunition in training engagements, and subjected their troops to small arms and artillery fire directed at them on a "near miss" basis.[6]

"Battle inoculation", as this rather frightening training method was called, had its drawbacks. The decision to train the British troops in populated rural areas of Norfolk proved to be disastrous. Troops and tanks were constantly damaging crops. Firing and explosions upset livestock.
In May 1942, a farmer was accidently shot dead as he drove his cattle onto marshland where the army trained for war. The terrible accident convinced the members of the British War Cabinet that it was best to relocate the actual training site.[7] In a bold move, the British purchased a stretch of inexpensive, resident-free land to the south of Hohenfels and drew up plans for a customised Nazi village to practise defeating the Germans.

As a diplomatic gesture, they hired a preservation specialist from Hohenfels to collaborate with their military architect in the planning stage.

3 Markt Hohenfels, ***Geschichte,*** *https://www.markt-hohenfels.de/6760-Geschichte.htm, n.d., last visit: 29.01.2024.*

4 Andreas Altenburger, ***Truppenübungsplatz Hohenfels,*** *https://www.lexikon-der-wehrmacht.de/Karte/Truppenubungsplatze/Hohenfels-R.htm, n.d., last visit: 29.01.2024.*

5 Andrew Levy, ***Good morning Afghanistan,*** *Daily Mail, 01.05.2009.*

6 Conal O'Donnell, ***Breckland Exodus – The Forced Evacuation of the Norfolk Battle Area 1942,*** *BBC, 11.11.2004.*

7 Ibid.

The team was to assure that the new battle village would fit seamlessly into the bullet ridden landscape.[8] The result was so convincing that even the German neighbours were fooled. The romantic array of two-storey farm buildings with steeped roofs, grouped around a central church with a cemetery, looked authentically Bavarian (see photo opposite page). Only a professional eye could detect an English hand in the composition of pastoral groups of oak and apple trees that embellished Eastmere's bucolic centre. Within four years, the recently founded Combat City had doubled its size.

The last few weeks of the Second World War brought chaos as allied forces sent a hail of bombs into Hohenfels. According to some accounts, the 300 man-strong "Freikorps of Adolf Hitler" abandoned the camp on the night of 22.04.1945.[9] Two weeks after the bombing the US army entered Hohenfels and occupied the city without resistance. The remaining soldiers were captured and the prisoners of war released. The material damage was severe, much of the infrastructure was rendered worthless.

By 1948 Hohenfels was demilitarised and reopened for settlement to war refugees and displaced persons. With infinite effort and hard work, the new settlers repaired the ruined buildings and began to plough the fallow land. Life returned to the village and a pacific period without gunshots began.[10] But peace did not last. The smouldering Korean crisis, and increasing tension with the former Soviet Union and its satellite states, had the US military government call for additional training facilities. Negotiations to take over and to remilitarise Hohenfels were met with noisy protest from the neighbouring communities, who were demanding the return of their properties that had been confiscated by the German Wehrmacht in 1938. They felt entitled to their homesteads, as the financial compensation had evaporated due to the war and the subsequent currency reform.[11] The wind finally dispelled their angry voices and the three months later the US army struck a deal.

The plan to re-found Combat City was ambitious. The entire training area was to be reorganised. The old wooden army barracks were to be demolished and replaced by a completely new, much larger settlement with stone buildings, lounges and a cinema. A department store and church were to be erected. The reconstruction triggered a hectic bustle everywhere. Timber traders from all over came to Hohenfels to buy

8 **MoD builds Afghan village in Norfolk,** Telegraph, 01.03.2009.

9 Andreas Altenburger, op. cit.

10 Markt Hohenfels, op. cit.

11 Paul Böhm, ***Wird Hohenfels wieder ein Truppenübungsplatz?***, Schmidmühlen.

Hohenfels during an urban assault training exercise with Canadian and American troops. The historic village has been used for combat training ever since the German Wehrmacht seized the town to prepare its troops for the Second World War. (Left)

Eastmere covers an area of approx. 700 × 300 m of fertile farming land. The historic town core wraps around the central village green, complete with graveyard and church. The occasional sheep can be found roaming among the 65 village buildings, many of which are shaded by ample trees. (Right)

and remove 200 has of forest to make place for the urban expansion. By 1951, six years after being declared occupied territory by the US Forces, Hohenfels reinvented itself as an American military training area.[12] Cattle breeding and farming was abandoned for good. In 1955, Germany joined the North Atlantic Treaty Organization (NATO), whose primary purpose was to unify and strengthen the Western Allies' military response to a possible invasion of Western Europe by the Soviet Union and its Warsaw Pact allies. US President Harry Truman's recommendation, to use military force to "contain" communist expansionism everywhere it seemed to be occurring, increased military spending four-fold.[13] The generous US budget raised the spirits in Hohenfels and facilitated a more open-hearted exchange with the neighbouring Eastmere. The British had been at a loss as to what to do next. Their victory lay six years back and Cold War tensions were running high. The uneasy wartime alliances – forged between the United States and Great Britain, on the one hand, and Great Britain and the Soviet Union, on the other – began to unravel. Hohenfels, now in American hands, offered financial aid if Eastmere was prepared to train together against the new enemy, the Soviets. The British were delighted. Additional buildings, newly paved roads and shared manoeuvre exercises made the two villages coalesce into a larger conurbation where the remnants of their different origins were barely distinguishable to the eye.

Some decades later, in 1980, an Israeli delegation paid a visit to the Hohenfels training district. The IDF considered "battle inoculation" to be a key issue in army drills and affirmed their interest in building a specific combat training facility for their troops. They had been training for years amid rickety shipping containers and cardboard cut-outs in the desert sun and urgently needed to upgrade their military work-out installations. The visiting Israelis hoped to obtain financial aid and build a proper, specific training ground within the boundaries of Combat City. The reception was positive and funds were generously granted by their American allies who were delighted about their new neighbours and within a few weeks, a central, suitable barren site had been reserved.[14] The founding stone for Baladia ("city" or "municipality" in Arabic) was laid in a solemn act and building work immediately commenced. For one month, 80 tractors worked ceaselessly to recreate a topography in which to situate a convincing Lebanese village.[15] Two months later Israel invaded Lebanon. The battlefield lessons were shared with their American friends who frequently came over to do combined training rounds.

12 *Markt Hohenfels, op. cit.*

13 *John L. Bisol,* We stood the watch, *p. 10, 2019.*

14 *Stephen Graham, op. cit., p. 193.*

15 *Barbara Opall-Rome,* Marines to train at new Israeli combat centre, *ePalestine Marine Corps Times, 26.06.2007.*

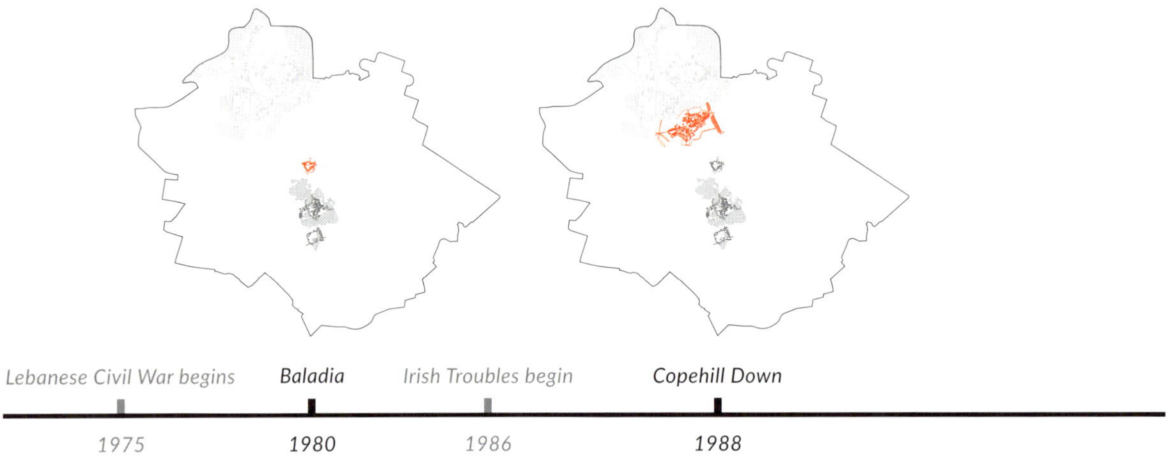

By 1988, the British Army decided that they needed to double their training capacity. "The Troubles", also known as the Northern Ireland conflict, had been enduring for 20 years and there was no end of violence in sight. The British military would need to step up their training in the specialised tactics of asymmetric warfare if they were to have any chance of winning the battle. They came to an arrangement with Combat City's ruling council and founded Copehill Down on the city's northern, wind-swept chalk plateau, a gunshot away from the Colony for the Feeble Minded in Muscatatuck. The new town was designed to look like a German village in the heart of Bavaria although the enemy to be battled was Irish. We do not know if the Bavarian vernacular architecture was chosen for symbolic reasons, based on perpetuating the powerful image of Germany as the enemy.[16] The geographical disassociation must have given some relief to British soldiers who prepared for battle at home without having to practise killing people like themselves in villages like their own.
The South German looking buildings were arranged around a sizeable, deceivingly romantic-looking village centre that included a graveyard. The strangely Protestant appearance of the church of Saint Jude's (the patron saint of lost causes) further heightened the cultural ambiguity of the district, a clear advantage in staging conflicts to come.[17]

The lively, oval-shaped Copehill Down stretches approx. 700 × 550 m across. Its 130 buildings, including a pub, a post office and a shop, are organised around the central square, lined by a hotel and a Protestant church. The train station is a ten-minute walk from the village square.

At the same time, the Americans were upgrading their installations in Hohenfels. Progress in combat techniques and scenarios required constant adaptions and obliged the city to live in a permanent state of renewal. Combat City, at this point, was an elaborate training backdrop of urban obstacles and hiding places. Apart from that, it was empty. No civilian obstructed the line of fire or caused distraction on the street. Military training staff at Hohenfels felt that a city without dwellers was neither accurate nor challenging in army terms and urged their superiors to add COBs (civilians on the battlefield) to the urban combat routine. They recommended the hiring of a specifically trained mock population of civilians that would work and live in the training villages as civilians. The actors were to receive role-playing instructions as well as civilian or military clothing.

At first the majority of COBs were recruited from retired army personnel, primarily those with combat experience. Most of the veterans recruited spoke a second language, and could draw on many skills to confuse or mislead the training troops in scenarios that included: "thieves" entering their base camp; "snipers" hiding among the population; pacifying angry

16 Berenice Baker, ***Tanks on the doorstep – the evolution of the military training village***, *Army Technology, 26.05.2014.*

17 *Ibid.*

DAILY
NEWSPAPERS
CIGARETTES
BREAD
MILK
ON SALE INSIDE

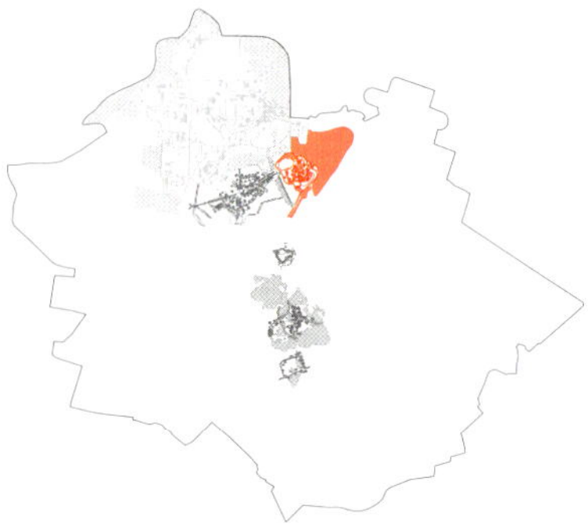

Lejeune — *1990*

Cold War ends — *1990*

Yugoslav Wars begin — *1991*

The moated Lejeune is surrounded by dense pine forest. The Bea Taylor Memorial Bridge is the principal access to the central church square of the settlement, which will finally occupy an area of some 1020 × 900 m. Amenities like a public fountain, picnic tables and the occasional chair make for a pleasant and relaxed visit.

mobs; and arresting bomb-toting "terrorists."[18] The experiment proved to be successful and petitions for a fake civilian population increased. To meet the rising demand, students, foreigners and unemployed locals were hired to enhance the Army's pool of COBs.

1990 was a busy year for Combat City. Building work in central Baladia was slow but steady. The Dutch and the French had looked at cheap land leases in the periphery and the recently inaugurated Copehill Down had boosted local construction activity. The US Marines had fallen in love with the pastoral charm of Copehill Down and wanted a version for themselves with a medieval moat as a distinguishing feature. Lejeune's construction plans had to be altered when the local commission denied building permission on copyright grounds and imposed a Mediterranean building style for the new American city district to match the French sounding name. Once the bureaucratic procedures were overcome, some of the densely wooded area to the west of Copehill Down was cleared to make way for Lejeune. Multilingual street signs were put up to give the district an international flair.[19] The core of Lejeune is comprised of 32 buildings that include a church, schools, petrol stations, hotels, homes and a partial sewage system. The town's high school includes a football field that happens to be perfect for landing a helicopter, and a gymnasium that doubles as a detention centre for prisoners of war.[20]

At the north-east boundary of Combat City, at the very end of a long narrow dirt road crossed regularly by sand dunes, a new district had sprung up.[21] For some years now, the dry and sandy plane at the end of the road had been used for aviation training. This district, Yodaville, began as little more than a target mark in the sand. By 1999, the US Marines felt that they needed a fully equipped air raid city to practise launching rockets, guns and laser guided missiles from all types of aircrafts. Flying had become a true and stimulating spectacle since the Gulf War had broken out nine years previously. For the first time, television included live news broadcasts from the front lines of the battle. The so-called "Video Game War" paid tribute to the continuous stream of images broadcast from cameras on board US bombers during Operation Desert Storm. The night time footage was disturbingly beautiful and perfectly detached from the horror and destruction on the ground. War had made prime-time television and all airborne military equipment was in demand to facilitate guilt-free, slick and high-tech entertainment. New pilots had to be trained and

18 GlobalSecurity.org, **Joint Multinational Readiness Centre (JMRC),** *www.globalsecurity.org/military/agency/army/jmrc.htm, n.d., last visit: 27.11.2018.*

19 Staff Writer, **Military Operations on Urban Terrain,** *https://bikersofamerica.blogspot.com/2015/04/usa-mout-military-operations-on-urban.html, 20.04.2015, last visit: 30.01.2024.*

20 **New MOUT Facility,** *Press release, Marine Corps Association, 1990.*

21 Ed Darack, **Welcome to Yodaville,** *Air & Space Magazine, 26.03.2009.*

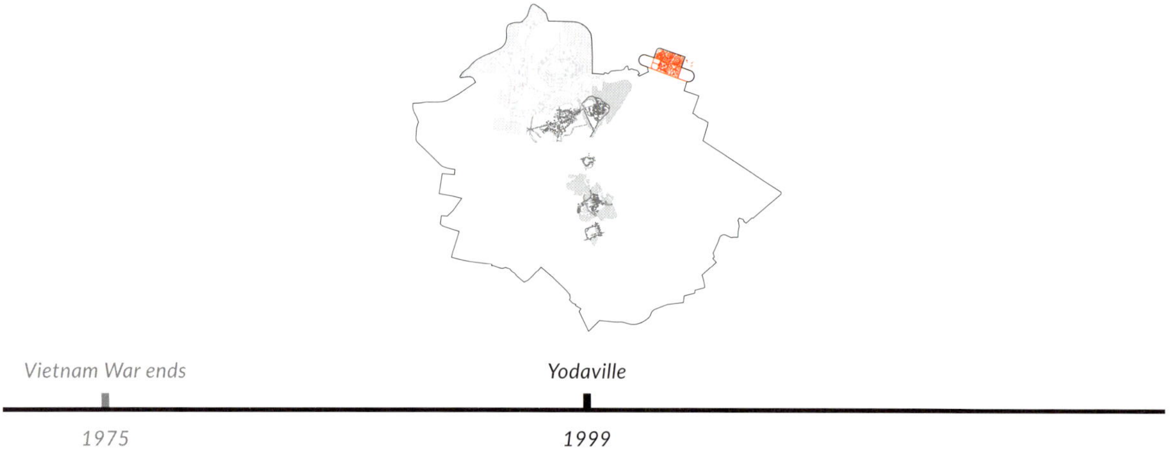

prepared for the complexities of promotional real-time transmission, which included alternating flight patterns and recalculating rocket launches for the benefit of high-resolution visuals to be broadcast on television.

The city planners did not shy away from the technical dataflow demands but showed unusual concern about environment issues. Financial calculations influenced military opinion towards sustainable urban planning solutions. Solemnly, city planners agreed to use only recycled material for the building of the new air Combat City. Yodaville was built from 23,000 cluster-bomb containers discarded during the Vietnam War.[22] Nearly 200 edifices, some 130 personnel targets, a large number of vehicles and many streetlights comprise the district. The buildings are organised in four sections of differing density and height that are connected by a radiating system of roads. The downtown section is represented by a number of high-rise buildings that are stacked in ziggurat fashion. Most tall structures are monolithic, but there is the occasional building that defies gravity with structurally audacious configurations and imposing façades. Pilots say that the district is convincingly urban.

The inauguration of Yodaville, including a lavish award ceremony for the "sustainable town construction prize", was overshadowed by the discovery of a human corpse. The first civilian casualty from the air raid raised a series of uncomfortable questions about the district's security. The ancient migrant route, on the east side of Yodaville, is still being used by illegal refugees in search for better living conditions. Border Patrol agents fear that the urban image of stacked containers illuminated at night will lure unsuspecting illegal immigrants in search of water into the bombing area. "When we track a group of illegals onto the range, we let the Marines know and they close down their operations", he explains. "This generally happens twice a week".[23] Unfortunately, many deaths are reported in this military exclusion area, where humanitarian aid – like food or even water – is impossible to deliver.[24]

The inhospitable Yodaville occupies some 700 × 275 m of desert sand. The intense heat distorts the vision of the 275 metal building blocks that comprise the town. Charred cars, tanks and human-shaped metal targets animate the streets, everything else falls from the sky.

22 *Stephen Graham, op. cit. p. 187.*

23 *Mark Shaffer,* **Yodaville Exists for Bombing Runs – Arizona's Newest Town Inviting Target,** *The Arizona Republic, 23.08.1999.*

24 *Rob O'Dell, Daniel González and Jill Castellano,* **Mass disaster at the border, little care in Washington D.C.,** *The Desert Sun, 15.12.2019.*

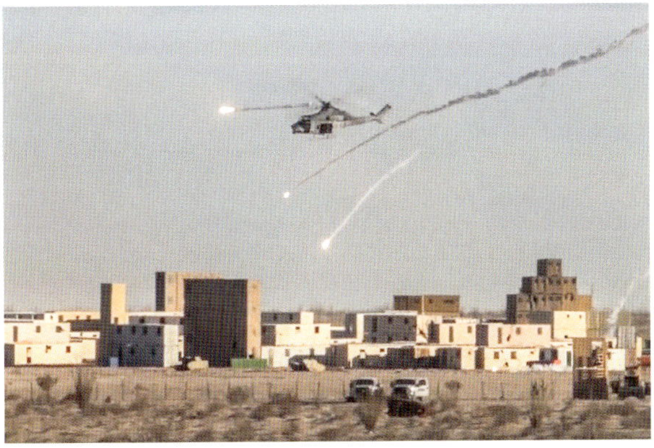

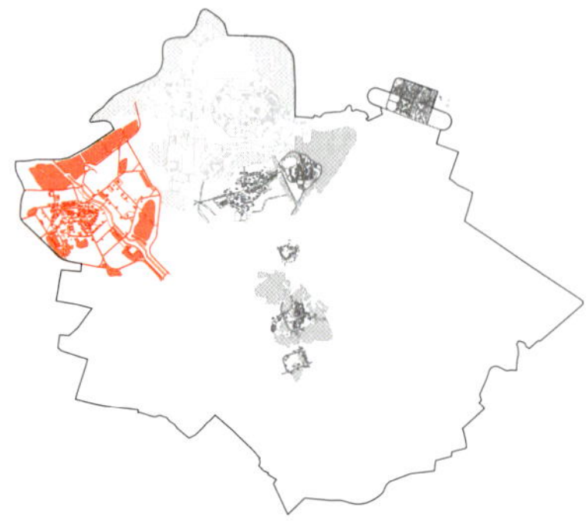

Urban Expansion

Yugoslav Wars begin — 1991

Marnehuizen — 2002

Combat City's expansion and growth is slow and intermittent, but fame has travelled beyond its boundaries. It was becoming increasingly fashionable (if dangerous) to move to Combat City.

When the Dutch decided to invest in a property that was not more than a few simple huts spread around a grassy plain, they were happy to know they were themselves far from Yodaville's deadly migrant route. The Dutch had haggled for years over costs versus gains, but by the beginning of the millennium, a suitable financial scheme materialised and plans were drawn up. They were delighted with their luscious green fields that were home to bird species such as skylarks, greylag harriers, rough-legged buzzards and short-eared owls. The only drawback was that the site lacked a proper forest.[25] The allegedly environmentally-friendly site preparations included the large-scale tree plantation (to conceal approaching troops rather than to offer nesting opportunity to the birds), the sowing of drought-resistant, slow-growing grass, as well as the lowering of groundwater levels to support the weight of manoeuvring tanks.[26] Unfortunately, the birds were unable to adapt to the noise and left when construction of Marnehuizen began.

Marnehuizen, the Dutch combat enclave, is located on the western border of Combat City. 150 Dutch training buildings in trendy 1950s vernacular style went up while the Yugoslav Civil War was being waged. The overall aspect of the suburban village with its church, town hall, train station, bank, school, petrol station and sixteen built ruins, resembles more a Dutch homeland scenario than a Bosnian village. Historic street signs that carry the names of roads bombed during air raids in Rotterdam at the beginning of the Second World War suggest that the official enemy remains German.[27] The streets are clean and fully equipped with telephone booths, portable toilets and waste containers. Marnehuizen has its own underground sewer system, a burial ground for eternal peace as well as a state-of-the-art LED lighting system. All buildings are wired and equipped with a dimmer system to control light pollution and guarantee Marnehuizen's ecological "Dark Sky Park" status.[28] Sometimes, a couple of confused red deer leave the new forest at first light before the morning mist has lifted, and cross the recently added "Afghan" cobblestone road in search of a way out.[29]

Marnehuizen is crossed by a meandering river and covers some 1,100 × 1,050 m of windy, green flatlands. Most of the family homes are painted in cheerful colours and sport a private back garden and garage. The city council, which presides over the central square, doubles as a Protestant church.

25 **Marnehuizen,** *www.plaatsengids.nl/marnehuizen, n.d., last visit: 29.01.2024.*

26 *Arthur van Beveren,* **Willem Lodewijk van Nassaukazerne,** *Defence Newspaper 14, 12.07.2019.*

27 *Elmar Keetman,* **Urban bulldog, Military machines international,** *08.2011.*

28 *Editor Noorderland,* **Mysterieus Marnehuizen,** *Noorderland, 12.05.2020.*

29 *Niek Stam,* **Laagvliegende kogels inarnehuizen,** *Reformatorisch Dagblad, 01.09.2009.*

Muscatatuck's active training farm with culturally "authentic" animals. (Left)

The bucolic setting of winding rivers and broad oak trees is a stark contrast to the decaying Muscatatuck. Eight of the 310 partially ruined buildings are submerged in the kidney shaped campus pond. A central clock tower keeps time for the smouldering decline. (Right)

Marnehuizen's inauguration ceremony was a great success, but a little further north, things were more than gloomy. The neighbouring Muscatatuck was going through bad times. Contemporary methods of mental illness treatment, together with time and death shrank its patient population from 3,000 down to twelve in 2001; by 2005 the mental asylum was entirely closed. The initial plan to raze the buildings and plant a tree farm were abandoned in favour of a Homeland Security training facility.[30] The Afghan War was well into its fourth year and military training was considered necessary. Within months, Muscatatuck's 1,000-acre landscape, including 200 existing brick structures, water reservoir and subterranean tunnels were turned into a live fire cyberwarfare training environment.

Muscatatuck is, together with Hohenfels, the only Combat City borough that is not custom built. This veteran district now specialises in disaster scenarios; its distinctive feature is its ruinous appearance. There was no need for reconstruction during its conversion from a psychiatric colony to an urban warfare training district. The original, solidly built art deco buildings make for perfect ruins. The 90-year-old hospital building has not been touched. Its disrepair and peeling paint make it a perfect prop for frequently held Afghan battle scenarios. One of the districts' oldest buildings, a former ballroom, has collapsed from neglect and enjoys frequent search-and-rescue missions within its walls. It also doubles as a sizeable Afghan home accidentally destroyed by an errant Air Force bomb.[31]

Rescue missions in collapsed structures and rubble extraction exercises require a townscape in ruins. Any architectural addition to the district is built as if destroyed: every new structure that goes up is designed to be collapsed. Parking garages, crammed with demolished cars, are engineered to look as though struck by an earthquake or hit by a bomb. Muscatatuck relies on donations to simulate chaos. Prefabricated concrete companies donate faulty material for the indispensable rubble piles on the street.[32] The recent addition of a specific multi-domain environment reflecting a 21st century battlefield is the only exception. The purpose-built cyberspace is spanking new, densely wired and full of digital gadgets. The black box simulates war scenarios on land, at sea, in air as well as in cyberspace. For increased realism, "human terrain" or "brown noise" (the military term for digital civilian presence) is added to the cyber game of war.[33]

30 *Stew Magnuson,* ***Indiana Psychiatric Institution transformed into urban training ground,*** *National Defense Magazine, June 2010.*

31 *Ibid.*

32 *Ibid.*

33 *Todd Harmeson,* ***EMA participates in #2018RoadtoRecovery exercise,*** *Madison County Emergency Management, 03.08.2018.*

BOATMAN RD

Low Budget
MOTEL

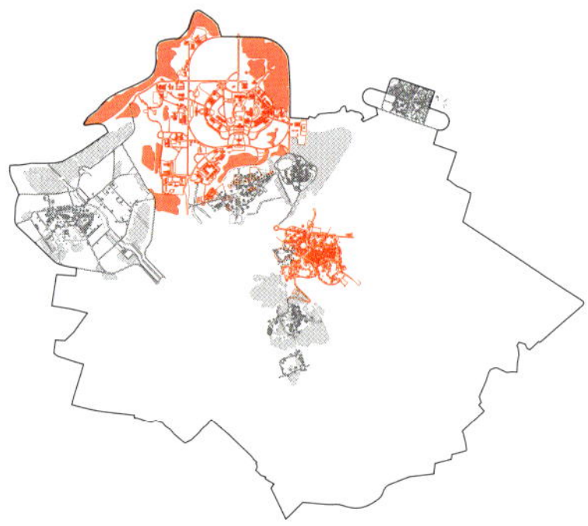

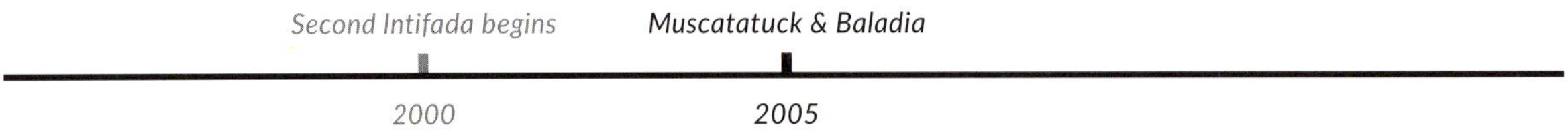

Muscatatuck authorities, delighted with the modern, cutting-edge addition to the ruined rubble-scape, glamorously re-christened the city district as Cybertropolis.

Despite its high-tech name, the most prominent feature of Cybertropolis remains the original, still active farm, where soldiers are trained to handle animals and crops, especially those found on Afghan farms. Culturally "authentic" animals and role-players add colour to the exercise scenarios and teach soldiers how to stay calm and stick to their mission amid the confusion of goats, sheep and chickens running loose in the market place. Some soldiers grow very fond of them. At the end of an exhausting training day, most will make their way to the farm – stroking animals helps combatants to relax. Sarahi, the camel, is often the centre of attention.[34]

The "axis of evil", a concept coined by George Bush after the attack on the World Trade Centre and used frequently to rally the American populace in support of the War on Terror, was firmly established by 2003. The capture or assassination of Osama bin Laden and Saddam Hussein had become US military priorities. Israel, America's great ally, had been training their special forces to assassinate Saddam Hussein in Tikrit for some time. Earlier, in 1992, Operation Bramble Bush was aborted and training suspended after five soldiers were killed during the rehearsal for the operation in Baladia.[35]

Ten years later, the Israeli Defence Forces launched Operation Defensive Shield during the course of the Second Intifada. The stated goal of the operation was to stop terrorist attacks. With Baladia's doors closed, the defence forces found themselves with nowhere to train. In a smart move, the army turned to a prominent Israeli real estate developer, who allowed the battalion to practise at night in one of his unfinished residential complexes.[36] The drill on built structures, with entryways, windows and elevator shafts turned out to be crucial for the outcome of the battle.

The military effort to control and pacify the city of Nablus in the northern West Bank had been conducted in an unconventional way. Rather than using the existing streets to get around, the soldiers blasted through walls and travelled through buildings to avoid sniper fire from above. During the battle, soldiers carved 100-meter-long tunnels out of a dense and contiguous urban structure. Although several thousand troops were manoeuvring

Five mosques call for prayer in the dense, hot desert settlement of Baladia. The size of its modern central square is as large as the adjoining, cramped bazaar, with its narrow alleyways. Even though Baladia is manageable in size – the district occupies some 630 × 730 m – exploring should be limited to the early hours of the day.

34 Staff Reports, **Small farm at military installation adds realism to training**, The Republic, 16.06.2018.

35 Eyal Weizman, **Walking through walls, Frontier Architectures**, Steidl, 2007.

36 Barbara Opall-Rome, **Marines to train at new Israeli combat centre**, Marine Corps Times, 26.06.2007.

Marines rehearse the military infestation strategy (breaking your way through the interior of buildings rather than travelling on the street) with avatars. (Left)

The orientalised Hohenfels, which stretches 450 × 400 m across, has grown to include minarets and a grand bazaar. Most of its building stock, some 80 structures, conserve their Bavarian look. Despite its new Afghan name, the market sells local produce and South German food. (Right)

simultaneously in the city, very few were visible from the air. They avoided streets, alleys, courtyards, any external doors, internal stairwells or windows and moved horizontally through walls and vertically through ceilings and floors. Unlike the Palestinians, the Israeli forces suffered few casualties in the raid. The military "infestation" strategy was heralded a great success and marked a clear shift in Israel's warfare doctrine.[37]

Baladia was reopened and construction work resumed on the district's solid and homogeneously grey, cubic and minimal buildings. The pre-fabricated concrete walls of the stark buildings include the novelty of built-in star shaped blast holes. By 2005 the district comprised a *kasbah*, a refugee camp, a downtown neighbourhood, a rural village section, a market area and plenty of urban outskirts. The dense urban environment is formed by some 500 structures with 1,200 doorways, 2,500 windows and multiple elevator shafts that are connected by many kilometres of paved streets and gravel roads. For added realism, charred automobiles and burned tires litter the roadways. In the near future, planners will add donkeys, sheep, dogs and other live animals that often provide early warning of approaching Israeli troops.[38]

The strategic move to take the soldiers off the street has had far reaching consequences. In urban warfare, all citizens are potential targets, because they happen to live in the same place as the enemy. With a bit of luck, they might stay out of trouble by avoiding public spaces. Under the new "infestation" doctrine, they will not even be safe at home. Military strategy has converted domestic interiors into thoroughfares and turned private living space into a battlefield. In military terms, civilians are but one more obstacle in the topography of combat. They are classified as human terrain and graphically represented as yet another layer of obstruction on the battle map.

Baladia's expansive borders were drawing closer to the boundaries of Camp Lejeune, located on its northern rim. Due south, the densely packed city began to encroach on Hohenfels, which, by December 2005, had been transformed into a Joint Multinational Readiness Centre called "Aghjabadi", the Bavarian replicate of Afghanistan, mosques included.[39] Relations between Baladia and Hohenfels were understandably complex, even tense, but common goals and a mutual enemy managed to diffuse most of the disputes and let pragmatism prevail.

37 *Eyal Weizman,* **Walking through walls, Frontier Architectures,** *Steidl, 2007.*

38 *Barbara Opall-Rome,* **Marines to train at new Israeli combat centre,** *Marine Corps Times, 26.06.2007.*

39 *Geographical imprecision –* **Aghjabadi is located in Azerbaijan and a fair shot from Afghanistan** *– seems not to affect military training.*

HOSPITAL
D85

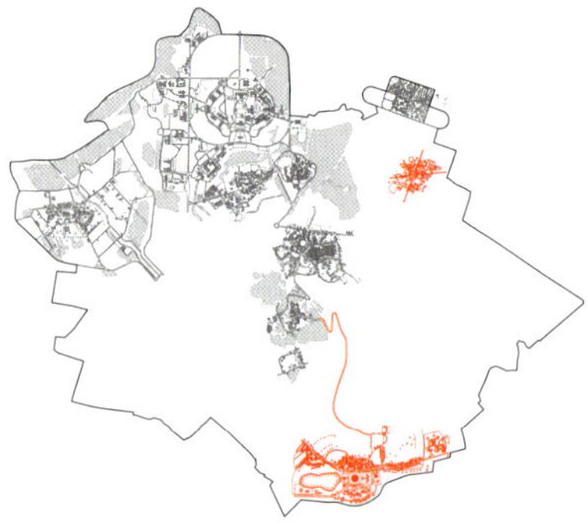

Afghan War begins	*Iraq War begins*	***Medina Wasl, Medina Jabal***
2001	*2003*	***2006***

Serious concerns about the unstable and unpredictable alliance between Aghjabadi and Baladia led the Americans to plan a brand-new Iraqi district, far from the troublesome city centre. They chose the exotic name of Medina Wasl for the new, very modest district in the sand blown plains to the north-east, just below the rather noisy aviation district of Yodaville. The economic advantages of using shipping containers as prime building material had already been verified by their neighbours. The same construction method was now to be applied in the peripheral district of Medina Wasl. Over the years, stone siding and decoration were added to the low-cost container units. Supplementary minarets and custom-made domes made the place more colourful and gave the new, rather humble neighbourhood a distinctive look.[40]

Medina Wasl's dusty roads converge in its large, central roundabout complete with hotel and mosque. The district's simple structures cover some 420 × 420 m of dusty terrain. Colourful domes and minarets compensate for the drab and unsightly buildings.

The majority of Medina Wasl's fake residents are poor; steady jobs are notoriously scarce. The major industry, a fictitious fertiliser plant, only employs the owner and his sons. An abandoned Borax mine sits silently on the hill overlooking the town. The district's urban layout is star-shaped; a radiating system of roads connects the 300 shed-like buildings that make up the town with an oversized central roundabout. The tank-proof traffic circle is flanked by a Sunni mosque, an international hotel (gift shop included) and a small hospital. A poor replica of the Princess of Hatra (a sandstone sculpture erected in 238 CE to protect the city of Al-Hadr, Iraq from Persian invaders) occupies the centre of the roundabout.

Sculptures and monuments are rare in Combat City. Maybe because warfare training leaves little time for contemplation, or because a monument on the battlefield is more likely to be used as a target than as a source of admiration. The concrete-coloured copy of the princess with a beehive turban enjoys the sturdy protection of concrete boulders and withered plants. A plaque at its base indicates that the sculpture was erected "in appreciation of the American Soldier, the true protector of democracy" by Strategic Operations, a San Diego based action/softcore adult film production company which was saved from near bankruptcy following 9/11 by entering the military simulation business.[41]

The simulation business was flourishing and many military contractors expanded and offered building solutions, atmospherics and role-players to animate the training scene. Hohenfels had been hiring COBs (civilians on the battlefield) for over 15 years. The primarily decorative function of

40 *Daniel Calder,* ***Iraqi village on Irwing,*** *United States Army, 31.03.2008.*

41 *D. Andy Rice,* ***Weaponizing Affect: A Film Phenomenology of 3D Military Training Simulations During the Iraq War,*** *Catalyst, Vol 2 No1, 2016.*

Muyuad, an Iraqi who role-plays the Iraqi Police Chief, in his room. He shares this shipping container with a roommate. (Left)

The busy, sprawling Medina Jabal spreads over a desert area of approximately 1,250 × 600 m. Its neuralgic centre, grouped around a boulder-like rock formation, is a colourful bazaar framed by a large roundabout which is surrounded by government buildings and an embassy. Some potted palms sway in the wind. (Right)

these actors was reassessed following shocking news reports of torture at Abu Ghraib prison in Iraq in April 2004. The US military dealt with the wave of public indignation by implementing "cultural awareness" training for all troops set to deploy to the Middle East. Role-players for training scenarios were now to be "culturally authentic" and teach the troops about their hopes, wishes, costumes and their dislike for torture. As a result, most of Medina Wasl's inhabitants are played by Iraqis and Afghans who fled their country and now participate in the war effort of their newly adapted home by representing themselves as the enemy.[42]

Saddam Hussein had been captured and his monument toppled by the marines. He was executed in December 2006. The power vacuum following Saddam's demise and the mismanagement of the occupation led to widespread violence, as well as a lengthy insurgency against US and coalition forces. To cater for the growing military training demand, plans for an upgraded and larger version of Medina Wasl were drawn up. The new Iraqi district by the name of Medina Jabal, was to occupy a strategic location on the southern border of the Combat City. Due to frequent seismic activity, the site was cheap and well protected from the desert winds by a large rocky mount. Its vicinity to the large dry riverbed of Wadi al-Sahara was another favourable factor. The design of Medina Jabal, based on satellite imagery of Baghdad, took longer than expected. The city council ruled against the initial low-cost shipping-container scheme and asked for greater authenticity. The newly founded Research and Development Centre worked closely with the engineers to ensure the construction design would be authentic to Iraqi standards and dimensions.[43]

Medina Jabal quickly developed from being a hamlet of wooden huts and gravel road to a sizeable neighbourhood, including a shanty town, a university, a police station, a prison complex, three mosques and some five km of tunnel systems. The busy town was quickly inhabited by 300 former homeless dwellers, who slept, cooked and ate in their shotgun-style shipping-container houses with portable latrines.[44] They dressed in costume and spoke three anti-American phrases in Arabic. They would, together with a group of hired real-life amputees, actively participate in the training sessions, adding intensity to the scenes of conflict and encouraging the soldiers to learn that every civilian was a potential terrorist and a hence a real threat to their lives.45 The set up was convincing and enjoyed great popularity. Its immediate success accelerated plans

42 Ibid.

43 Daniel Calder, **Iraqi village on Irwing,** United States Army, 31.03.2008.

44 Scott Magelssen, ***Rehearsing the "Warrior Ethos", Theatre Immersion and the Simulation of Theatres of War,*** Project Muse, March 2009.

45 Derek Gregory, ***Sim Cities and Theatres of War,*** Geographical Imaginations,19.05.2013.

163

2

Resting after the morning prayer in the outskirts of Wadi al-Sahara. (Left)

It takes a ten-minute walk from the town centre to reach Lejeune's new Afghan district in the woods. A makeshift mosque is the spiritual centre of the dark and isolated container village. (Right)

for expansion with an eventual total of 600 buildings. The ambitious programme, launched in 2007, included plans to increase the population from around 250 to 1,000, boost the number of animals and, as a novelty, incorporate children.[46]

Halfway between Medina Jabal and Baladia, on the western banks of the dry riverbed, which is shaded by 29 palm trees, large columns of construction trucks moved in and out of what was to be the new town of Wadi al-Sahara. Throughout 2005, millions of dollars were expended on an ambitious construction project that was to resemble yet another Iraqi town.[47] By the end of 2006, Wadi al-Sahara already boasted 200 finished homes, including government buildings, a village centre, business areas, residences and a mosque. Most of them are made from stacked-up metal cargo containers fitted with doors, windows and external stairs. Small gold and metallic blue mosque domes protrude above the rooftops.[48] The dirt streets are marked with signs in Arabic. Here and there, burned-out cars provide the décor of war. Acting residents play their part amid the dust, some representing elected officials, others unemployed individuals, businessmen, utility workers, civil servants or security forces. Their religious inclinations are also part of the script; Wadi al-Sahara dwellers follow the same creed as the enemy in the far-away Al Anbar Province of Iraq.

Disastrous results in Afghan or Iraqi theatres of war drew attention to the insufficient preparation and lack of on-site knowledge of the invading soldier. To correct this trend, intensive pre-deployment training for all military personnel became a priority. Four-week training programmes were designed and drawn up, everyone was expected to be exposed to long and sleepless battle scenes. On January 2007, Bush publicly announced an Iraqi troop surge called "the new way forward". An extra 20,000 men were to be deployed to Baghdad and the Anbar Province and needed to be prepared. Combat City was in great demand and prices to build or to train were at an all-time high. Construction activity was frantic, qualified labour short and building material scarce. Most contractors had no other choice than to opt for standardised, low-cost container modules to control expenditure and ensure supply for their building sites.

Lejeune had big expansion plans and needed to update the simulation of the enemy town by adding an Afghan district to its Mediterranean village. It was common knowledge that the local top brass had a weakness for

46 Scott Magelssen, ***Rehearsing the "Warrior Ethos", Theatre Immersion and the Simulation of Theatres of War,*** *Project Muse, March 2009.*

47 Nicholas J. Schlosser, ***U.S. Marines and Irregular Warfare: Training and Education, 2000–2010,*** *United States Marine Corps Quantico, 2015.*

48 Mark Muckenfuss, ***Marines train in mock Iraqi village at Twentynine Palms combat centre,*** *Leatherneck, 26.12.2008.*

Afghan War begins	*Iraq War begins*	*Wadi al-Sahara, Chinchilla, Anaconda*	*KASOTC*
2001	*2003*	*2007*	*2009*

distinguished names and no one was surprised when "Nisr min Al-Bahar" or Eagles from the Sea was chosen for the extension.[49] Despite its fancy name, the built reality is far from glamorous. The entire district is constructed from stacked shipping containers and is visually closer to a prison camp than an Afghan village. The modules are one to three storeys tall and include indoor and outdoor stairwells and ladders. None of the 100 buildings are fixed to the ground, meaning the environment can be freely rearranged to suit new enemies or training operations. The dreary look and lack of character is compensated by specially recorded ambient sound. The entire area is wired with speakers that reproduce the call to prayer, noises of chirping birds, barking dogs, as well as the cluttering noise of everyday life in the village. Iraqi nationals will be contracted to roam the streets as locals or to play insurgents.[50] Some of the COBs are equipped with realistic blood packs that pour, once activated, rivers of blood from a fake wound.

The roofless village of Chinchilla covers a modest area of 450 × 200 m. It lines the intersection of dirt roads that are primarily used by armoured vehicles. Sightseeing is challenging as half of the 75 village structures are surrounded by protective walls.

Other options to deal with high prices and shortage of building supply were being explored. The Spanish, short of money, had come up with a singular low budget scheme. They decided to build their entire training village with a cost efficient, roofless construction method. Chinchilla (furry rodent in Spanish), is a growing cluster of roofless concrete block buildings, huddled alongside Medina Wasl's western arterial road, right next to "Nisr min Al-Bahar". The unpretentious village with a North African air is lined with a large number of cast iron streetlights, salvaged from an abandoned speculative housing scheme nearby. They are merely symbolic, comforting perhaps, as there is no electric system to run them on. As a result, no light is being shed on the surprising number of snakes, scorpions, tarantulas and black spiders moving around the dusty training ground.[51]

The Spanish enthusiasm for helicopter training is comprehensible considering the hazardous ground conditions of their new training district. Airborne access and vertical movement through buildings is an essential part of urban combat training and Chinchilla is an ideal training ground. As time is crucial in surprise assaults, troops are taught how to climb swinging ropes in record time while hanging from the helicopter. Pilots practise hovering low over the roofless village in order to drop their troops straight into the buildings. They must learn how to avoid drones and falcons during the operation and how not be distracted by the unsettling noise of helicopter blades slicing through thick clouds of Moroccan locusts swarming the

49 Cpl. Brandon Holgersen, **Mobile urban training facility unveiled,** Lejeune Marines Mil, 03.04.2007.

50 Ibid.

51 **Centros de adiestramiento y campos de maniobras y tiro,** Revista Ejército n. 800 extraordinario, p. 34, November 2007.

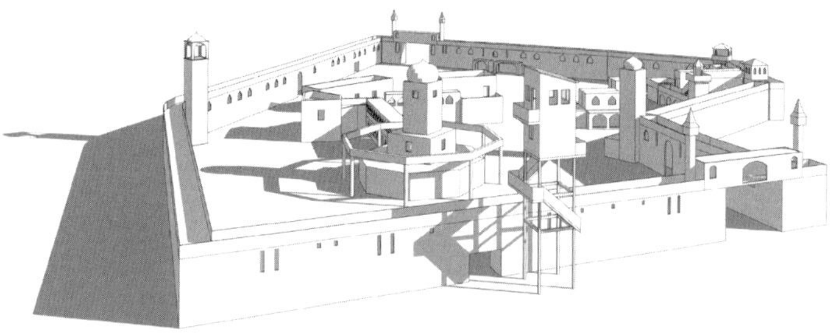

Anaconda is the smallest and the most secreted of Combat City's districts. Visitors must travel through long stretches of dense woodland to catch a glimpse of the gilded domes and spires within the city walls.

area throughout the day.[52] Spanish pilots, due to their experience in these difficult conditions, are frequently asked to participate in Iraqi helicopter missions.[53] On their return they share their combat experience and military insight with their new American neighbours who are only too keen to learn all about the art of "fast rope insertion".

The US Army, with the mythical gold-laden Fort Knox as their home base, constructed a new, walled container city by the name of Anaconda right next to Chinchilla's roofless housing estate. Its defensive walls protect a surprisingly ornate town with plenty of oriental details. Pink painted ship-containers with custom-made pointed arch windows and minaret tower extensions simulate Afghan conditions. Even the proper citywall traces a sinuous Arab *ogee* curve on the ground. Little is known about the walled city; it does not figure in any military annuals or other official reports, and extensive research has yielded nothing. Clandestine training videos and satellite images are the only visual proof of its mysterious existence.

The Jordanians devised a different scheme to supplement their tight budget. They could neither afford to build what was going to be their own modern town district with matching airport, nor pay for its maintenance. In 2009, King Abdullah II personally acquired a rocky canyon on the eastern periphery of the combat town and convinced his American allies to pay for the Jordanian construction.[54] KASOTC became the first rental district in Combat City to generate its own income. The solidly built town - designed in contemporary Middle Eastern style - is for lease to anyone willing to pay. It not only offers a base for training of international Special Forces and Jordanian border guards but also for military adventure holidays, corporate leadership programmes, and stunt training for actors.[55] KASOTC's setting is its major asset. A large number of rectangular, earth-coloured buildings fill the twisting hollow of the abandoned mine and offer unprecedented opportunities for live fire exercises within its high canyon walls (see central image on page 43). The sound of gunfire echoes off the steep limestone cliffs, while fog generators and rooftop explosions generate an adrenaline filled atmosphere - much to the delight of the troops and terror of the occasional sheep on a nearby bluff.

For promotional purposes, the district organises annual "Counterterrorism Olympics", where special operation forces and law enforcement teams from around the globe compete against one another in a test of skill and

52 Ibid.

53 Josechu Guillamon, **550 militares se forman en el Cenad antes de ir a Irak,** La Tribuna de la Ciudad Real, 14.10.2018.

54 Josh Eells, **Sleep-away camp for postmodern cowboys,** NY Times, 19.07.2013.

55 Benjamin Schuetze, **Jordan's KASOTC: Privatising anti-terror training,** Al Jazeera, 17.06.2017.

endurance. The event is sponsored by international weapons producers who, in turn, showcase their products to the participating units.[56] (This mutually beneficial arrangement will be copied by the Germans to finance the construction of Schnöggersburg a few years later). Other popular attractions in the district include hijack workouts in an authentic airplane and lessons in counter-terrorism and irregular warfare tactics. The famous dual-purpose dog race to detect narcotics and explosives appeals to many. These cross-functional dogs are sold to the highest bidder after about 90 days of onsite training.[57] Regular events include weapon trade fairs, an international air show, a permanent military arms bazaar and frequent kidnap training. Needless to say, KASOTC is booked out many years in advance.

Meanwhile, in Afghanistan, Taliban insurgents, far outgunned and outnumbered by the allied forces, successfully continued their asymmetric warfare with guerrilla raids, suicide attacks and turncoat killings. NATO responded by increasing troops for counter-insurgency operations, ordering programmes to “clear and hold” villages and “nation building” projects in order to win the hearts and minds of the enemy. The troops were instructed to kill less and help more, which led to a lot of confusion in the military ranks. Anthropologists and cultural specialists were sent to help with the task. But enemy hearts resisted and violence sharply escalated. By mid-February 2009, Barack Obama announced that 17,000 additional men would be deployed to Afghanistan.

The English prepared for the upcoming Iraqi troop surge with a remarkable urban transformation plan. The central Nazi village of Eastmere, custom-built during the Second World War, was now to be transformed into an Afghan town by the name of Ishmara. Scores of brand new L-shaped, flat-roofed courtyard dwellings tripled the size of the orientalised town. Perimeter mud walls “Afghanised” the original buildings in its centre, supplementary alleyways, maize fields and a bustling market place completed the cultural transformation. The sounds of prayer emitted from the mosque travel far beyond the city core. Even the rural population on the southern periphery organises their daily business according to the muezzin. Most live in concrete-clad single-storey compounds, interlinked by high-walled alleys. Each compound contains between four and twelve homes decorated with rugs and arranged around a courtyard with a vegetable patch, a well and a washing-line. Roughly 8,000 props are deployed

The rural Ishmara is the Afghan expansion of the Eastmere district. The re-creation of Helmand’s operational theatre feels out-of-place in the grey, damp Norfolk plain.

KASOTC winds through 1,600 × 900 m of rocky gorge. Its 150 buildings, airport included, sit tightly packed in an abandoned mine. Winding roads, ideal for car chase training, connect the different battle zones with the hotel. (Right)

56 Ibid.

57 Linda Hindi, ***KASOTC: State-of-the-art special operations training***, *The Jordan Times, 08.06.2014.*

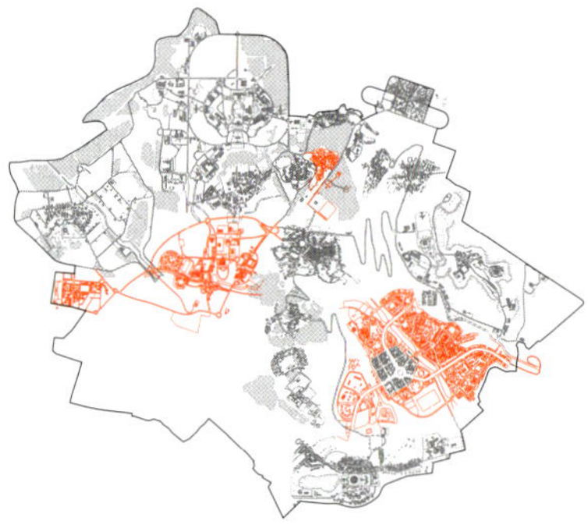

Wadi al-Sahara, Camp Lejeune, Jeoffrécourt, CTZUB

2011

to replicate the sounds, smells and traditional Afghan trappings. These inclusions complete the stage for military lessons on winning hearts, defusing improvised explosive devices and building better relationships with the locals.

The year 2011 began with several events significant to the development of Combat City. The Arab Spring brought tension to the southern Mediterranean. The Pakistani Spring was marked by the assassination of Osama bin Laden. Unrest in Syria escalated to an armed conflict after protests calling for the removal of Bashar al-Assad were violently suppressed. Further to the south, Yemen's political crisis was building fast. Two months before the spring unrests, American military gathered in large numbers to celebrate the completion of Wadi al-Sahara, by now the largest and most elaborate Combat City district. It had expanded all the way to the rocky beds of KASOTC and spread north to connect directly to Baladia. Its southern fringes now blended smoothly into the periphery of Medina Jabal, creating a single, continuous urban fabric that extended all the way to rural Ishmara to the west.

Wadi al-Sahara had developed into a dense, urban area with the capacity to accommodate the training of up to 15,000 marines and sailors simultaneously.[58] Most of its 1,200 buildings are made from prefabricated metal containers of all colours and sizes. Central, representative buildings are built in solid concrete. The visual impact of Wadi al-Sahara is radically modern in its simple utilitarian building style; there are no concessions made for decorative or culture-specific detail. Architecturally, Wadi al-Sahara embodies a type of minimal combat building style that has found many followers and is rapidly extending throughout the city. The lack of folkloric detail in representation of the enemy is compensated by the use of smell generators and acoustic embellishment as well as its numerous, diverse population. Markets, hotels and buildings are manned with Iraqi actors. Some 900 of them, representing civilians, officials and insurgents, live and work alongside the practising marines. It is their job to expose the troops to the chaos and stress of close combat and to gently but firmly remind them that being polite is considered to be the new force-protection priority. After the inauguration ceremony, guests watched tanks, amphibious vehicles and marine infantry in a battle exercise in the town. Amid the distant boom of artillery, the crackle of automatic weapons and the flash of explosives, the troops suffered their first casualty. A two-year old

Wadi al-Sahara's vast footprint covers some 1,500 × 1,350 m of desert sand. It is not a place for walking. The scale of its unpaved roads is suitable for marching troops and large convoys of tanks. There is no place to sit and rest. The buildings provide no shade and there is no foliage to be found.

58 Bryan Finoki, ***MOUT urbanism,*** *https://subtopia.blogspot.com/2008/02/mout-urbanism.html. last visit: 02.06.2018.*

bomb-sniffing dog, a Labrador Retriever that had been training for deployment to Afghanistan later in the year, was killed when it came too close to a detonated explosion.[59]

Lejeune, further north, was also unveiling its second, sizeable extension. The European-looking village had recently been enlarged with a sprawling Afghan container neighbourhood called the Eagles from the Sea. Lejeune's second expansion was experimental. The construction of the new neighbourhood, called "Camp Devil Dog", was to be a training programme in itself. This way, combat engineers would get to practise their construction skills before having to build in hostile areas on deployment.[60] The forest that separated Lejeune from the roofless Spanish village was cleared by fellow soldiers and the combat engineers went to work. Gradually the DIY village filled the gap between the two neighbourhoods of Lejeune. The new concrete block buildings are designed with wooden sash windows and external metal stairs, the combination of which gives them a melancholic retro air. Lack of time and know-how resulted in many roofless structures. Only the best construction teams managed to roof their buildings, plaster their façades and fit windows and doors. However, the result is convincingly urban and nobody worries too much about the unfinished buildings. Roofless architecture is quickly becoming a distinguishing mark of this part of town.

The Dutch began to feel impatient with the French. Their joint venture agreement had been signed 16 years ago. Both had shared the nightmare of failing to protect Srebrenica and avoid the slaughter of thousands of Bosnian Muslims in the Yugoslav War. Europe's deadliest conflict since the Second World War had raged on for years and cost more than 140,000 lives. In one of their bilateral meetings during the Kosovo War, both nations decided to learn from their mistakes and be better prepared by investing in specific urban warfare training facilities. The Dutch suggested they acquire suitable terrains in Combat City and praised the benefits of sticking together. The French agreed and both parties began work on financial resources and suitable designs. The Dutch finished Marnehuizen by 2002. It would take the French an extra ten years to complete their part of the deal. The reasons for the delay were twofold. The construction plan was very ambitious and the technical difficulties in the preparation of the ground were plentiful.[61] The French had chosen to buy the central plain, mainly for its flat terrain and strategic position

It's an easy stroll heading east from Lejeune's moat to the newly installed Camp Devil Dog. The orderly, well-lit neighbourhood unfolds along sinuously winding streets. Arabic street signs and small bazaars add an exotic flare to Western-style sash-window apartment buildings.

59 Kelly O'Sullivan, **Base unveils $170 million urban warfare training facility**, Hi-Desert Star, 26.01.2011.

60 Pfc. Jackeline Perez Rivera, **Combat engineers build Forward Operating Base for Camp Devil Dog**, U.S. Marines Article, 28.09.2011.

61 Juliette Demey, **When the army plays war**, Gratiane de Moustier, 22.01.2019.

The theatrical CTZUB comprises 40 built structures. Tall architectural props, mock ruins and snaking trenches create an evocative combat stage that covers some 300 × 500 m of horizontal terrain. The elevated watchtower on the northern corner of the battlefield provides a scenic view and is the safest place for contemplation.

within the community. However, when the first bulldozers moved in, unexpected hidden treasures of prior warfare came to light. Tons of combat debris such as landmines, grenades, rockets, shells and explosives from both World Wars contaminated the grounds and posed a serious threat to the community.[62] The clearing and decontamination delayed the construction phase of Jeoffrécourt which, on completion, was big enough to shelter 5,000 people.

The Dutch felt exposed at their borders to the west, south and east and did not get along with their only neighbour to the north. The orderly, nature-loving Dutch, who organised regular boy scout camps in their district, could not get used to the loud, messy, gadget-driven "Cybertropolis". Cybertropolis had added disaster-training facilities to their installations. The newly built "destroyed" structures were near completion: abandoned cars, broken concrete and piles of rubble gave the setting a dystopian touch. The Dutch expressed their environmental concerns but were only laughed at by their shoddy neighbours.

So they called the French and reminded them of their commitment.
To speed things up and bridge the construction delay of Jeoffrécourt, the Dutch offered them an interim lease of an uncontaminated building site on their southern border, where construction could begin immediately. The French seized the opportunity and decided to erect an experimental shooting district with the bureaucratic sounding name of CTZUB. The innovative city plan has very little in common with the neighbouring Dutch village vernacular. CTZUB is designed and built for the sole purpose of firing live munition. Its buildings are compressed into large, multi-storeyed strips with only a corridor as interior space. The zigzagging façades are lined with long rows of windows and archways that offer strategic views and shooting angles of the urban ensemble and beyond. The urban layout is classic, its visual effect theatrical. Carefully planned perspectives and overlapping layers of stark concrete structures and wooden lined walls create an urban landscape similar to a ruined city. These are ruins in which to shoot and be shot at. Despite its exquisite aesthetics, the setting is highly practical. One week of repairs is scheduled after every third rotation. Bullets have to be dug out of wooden walls and panels which, iddled with metal shells, are subsequently replaced. Everything is monitored, wired and ready for replay. Small screens inform soldiers if they have been hit, seriously injured or have died. In the latter case,

62 *Halima Najibi*, ***Sissonne: explosion d'une demi tonne de munitions***, *France3 TV, 30.10.2014.*

they must either lie on the floor for five minutes waiting to be evacuated by their comrades, or remove their helmet to indicate that they are dead and should be left behind.[63]

While everyone was trying to not get killed in CTZUB, progress was being made in Jeoffrécourt. Clearing and decontamination had been finalised. The artificial riverbed, including a harbour basin and water navigation locks, had been dug out and building construction was well on its way. The town's footprint is far more conventional than its pistol-ridden counterpart, but in terms of size and urban diversity, it is unmatched. The architectural language is generic French with a Central European touch. Jeoffrécourt represents a classic homeland setting, ideal for training domestic troops in how to fight the enemy on home turf. The four areas of Jeoffrécourt spread over more than 250 acres. The river connects the old town with the suburban area to its west and the high-rise housing estate to the east. A large commercial area occupies the plain northern area of the district. The narrow streets of the historicised city centre are organised around a large town hall square, with the church and train station in walking distance. The rest has to be done by car. Large arterial roads connect the low-income banlieues with the typically depressing industrial estate and residential sprawl beyond. The buildings are solid and well put together (French army brass claims Jeoffrécourt to be entirely tank-proof) but has no interior finishes. There are frequent complaints from the trainees about the lack of proper beds and heating in winter.[64]

The complaints about difficult living conditions are similar to the ones in the German Schnöggersburg, the big, new neighbour to the south. Construction of the state of the art combat town had begun the same year Jeoffrécourt opened its doors. Six years later, the first section was blessed by a Christian military chaplain and officially opened with stately honours.[65] The ritual raised some uncomfortable questions about Christian ethics, but the dignitaries turned a deaf ear and pushed on. They were keen to watch the first of many battles in what was to be the superlative of all urban warfare training environments. Schnöggersburg has everything one could wish for: its planning is meticulous, its execution flawless and the construction standards high. The town, which seems to have been cast in one mould, is somewhat eerie in its grey, standardised perfection. Schnöggersburg has a German look, its building typology mirroring a homeland territory with a subtle Eastern European air. The result is so

It is a ten-minute drive to Jeoffrécourt from CTZUB. A bridge connects the central square, on the north bank of Jeoffrécourt's narrow waterfront, with the temple quarter on the south side of the channel. Pedestrians should be cautious when crossing the bridge; tank traffic is surprisingly common.

63 Alix Valenti, **Preparing for Battle,** Armada International, 19.09.2017.

64 Nicolas Montard, **Jeoffrécourt, ville factice de l'armée française,** L'édition du soir, 09.03.2016.

65 Steve Przybilla, **Eine Stadt für den Kriegsfall,** Neue Zürcher Zeitung, 21.11.2017.

39

RESTAURANT

Schnöggersburg

2018–2021

convincing that serious doubts about its authentic purpose have been raised. To the uninformed eye, the Bundeswehr could be preparing for military action within its national limits, specifically outlawed by the German constitution. The official statement, that there is no fear of civil war conditions to justify homeland battles at this point in time, did not do much to disperse public concern.[66] After the Second World War, deployment of German soldiers abroad was out of bounds; the Bundeswehr served as a purely defensive army. Its first military operation under UN mandate was during the civil war in Bosnia-Herzegovina in 1995. Four years later the highly controversial participation in the Kosovo War relaunched the German troops in direct battle duty. They continued from thereon. Having deployed in Afghanistan, Sudan, Somalia, Mali and in the Mediterranean, they felt that their time had come to have a proper training city.

A stroll along the riverbank promenade is a safe way to discover Schnöggersburg. The central canal divides the district in half. Three of a total of five bridges connect the city halves, the remaining two crossings lead into open heath.

They developed an elaborate and clever financing plan to fulfil their ambitious aspirations and made a deal with a giant German armament firm who agreed to finance the entire operation. In turn, the private operator would lease the terrain and the technology to the army. The chance to test their weapons and war machinery on site (before selling them to the very army that was being trained to use them) was a lucrative spin off. With financial matters resolved, the Germans went on to buy a suitably large site in Combat City. Remembering their own experience, the French neighbours suggested they first search the chosen terrain for hidden debris of war before signing the lease. They reminded the Germans that the rain drenched heath they had led their eyes on had been cleared by the Wehrmacht to establish their artillery shooting range back in 1934. After the German defeat in the Second World War, Soviet troops had taken over the vast flatlands and used it as manoeuvre grounds. The Russians left in 1994, four years after the German reunification. The French were convinced that the site was as contaminated as their own. Surprisingly, the scrutiny of the soil did not unearth any toxic waste, just a few rusty tank chains, building rubble and an old hunting map which served as inspiration for the place and street names of the new town.

Schnöggersburg's construction plans are ambitious; the aim to accommodate 2,500 soldiers as well as 500 COBs by 2021 seems more than realistic. A total of 16 km of roads, from gravel lanes to an urban four-lane expressway, are to connect town squares of every size and colour to practise crowd control. As there are no natural waters on the terrain, an artificial

66 *Schnöggersburg – modernstes Übungszentrum des Heeres,* Bundeswehr Journal, 18.10.2018.

An aerial view of the central bridge crossing the river Eiser in Schnöggersburg and its elaborate, sacred multi-faith building on the western bank.

river was built to accommodate five mobile bridges. Underground tunnels and sewerage systems provide training opportunities for moving through the city without being seen. Above ground facilities include a railway station as well as a working water plant, a power station and a sports arena. A chemical factory has been erected to simulate risks originating from that industry. An area of destroyed infrastructure and slums defines the northern periphery designed for special threats. In comparison, the agricultural area with quaint suburbs to the south seems almost bucolic. But the appearance is deceptive. Most family homes are equipped with shoot-through-wall capabilities, special visual effects and pyrotechnic capacities. The high-tech warfare gadgets are yet to be installed downtown. The city, halfway through construction, is a dull, high-rise district with residential and commercial buildings including a bazaar and Western-style shopping arcade. The hospital and a Koran school are located in the same area. The church, the synagogue and the mosque rise close to the old town with its narrow streets. The townhouses are solidly built, but lack, as in the case of the French, any domestic commodities or interior fittings. Only 19 of the 500 buildings are frost-free and ready to be used as overnight accommodation.

The Russians were less fussy about low temperatures and uncomfortable lodging. Their Defence Ministry had placed an order for a training centre with the German Armament Cooperation years ago. The facility was to be similar to Schnöggersburg, with greater emphasis on simulation-supported training. The Russians felt that virtual training was a realistic means of preparing troops, with the added advantage of reducing fuel consumption as well as protecting heavy equipment from wear and tear. Relations went sour over the Ukraine crisis in 2014 and the deal had to be called off before completion. A few months later, the German Armament Cooperation announced that a new customer from the Middle East had placed an order for a comparable facility. Rumour has it that tentative land deals are being discussed with the Medina Jabal district authorities. If these talks were to prosper, Combat City would extend towards the south and further reinforce the cities' characteristic east-west divide.

Combat City currently covers over 9.3 million m^2 of territory. Its predictions for the future, considering the conflicts to come, are optimistic.

THE CONTEMPORARY CITY

Built to practise the art of war, Combat City is a set of elaborate, life-size replicas of enemy towns, designed to acclimatise soldiers to the place they will invade. Despite its contradictions, the sum of displaced and reimagined urban scenarios has grown into a tightly woven city plan of considerable dimensions. Combat City is the biggest training ground of its kind and famous for its cultural variety and adaptability to adverse conditions. The ethnically diverse city spreads over an area of 9.3 km^2 and has a capacity to shelter almost 50,000 inhabitants.[1] The generous flow of revenue from armament and military contracts maintains the city's economic health and provides numerous job opportunities. Soldiers, actors and mechanics from over 50 countries come to live, work and fight here. During the busy tourist season, over 17,000 visitors-in-arms descend on the city's streets and increase the population by a third.

Each of the city's 17 districts offers unlimited opportunities to practise conquering a foreign city at home. Each neighbourhood represents a particular enemy by means of a corresponding reconstructed city fragment. The borough of Medina Wasl, for instance, was designed to prepare the troops for the Iraqi war. The district's footprint is based on a satellite image of Baghdad; its meandering streets, large squares and the *kasbah* area, imitate fragments of the enemy's capital.[2] The city district of Baladia, in contrast, mirrors a Palestinian urban environment, while Eastmere enlarged its borders in rural Afghan style. The resulting collage of relocated city fabric, urban overlays, mirror images and reinterpretations of the "other" has come to be the distinguishing characteristic of the town.

The city's image is complex, its workings adaptable. As new conflicts arise and enemies change, the town alters its look, exchanges players and adjusts its daily routine. Combat City is not a simple backdrop for conflict, nor its mere consequence, but a dynamic field locked in a feedback-based relationship with the diverse forces operating within it: residents, soldiers, enemies, actors, robots and unspecific agents. The population's enactment of the scenarios, dislocated in space but not in time, makes the city into a unique, dynamic mirror of a world in arms.

1 *See* **Combat City plan** *on page 54.*

2 *Daniel J. Calder,* **Iraqi Village on Irwin**, *army.mil publications, 31.03.2008.*

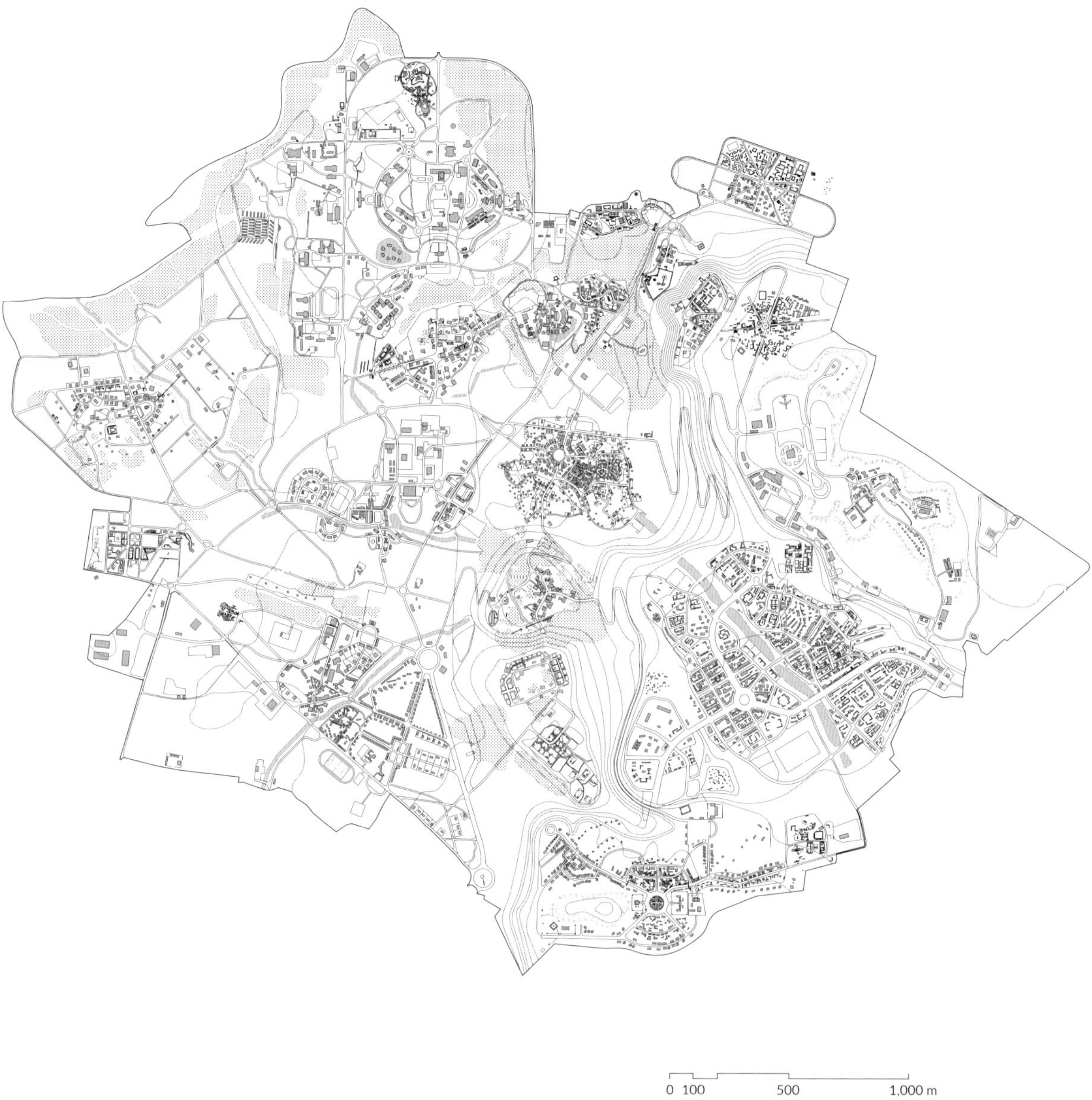
0 100 500 1,000 m

Topography and Climate

The city's geographical situation is as extraordinary as its purpose. Prehistoric grinding of tectonic plates fractured the land to create an abrupt transition between the flat western plane and the eastern highland. The mountainous interior, with its jagged peaks and high plateaus, breaks unexpectedly as steep cliffs give way to woodland and fertile plains. The craggy mountain ridge follows the line of the big geological fault, which runs from north to south and divides the city in half. The disruptive topography is the result of a tectonic fracture that continues to produce unsettling seismic waves.[3]

The western half of the city is built on flat land. Green fields gradually rise from sea level to meet the central cliff at 250 m of altitude. Until the army moved in most of the area was covered by woodland. Trees were felled to improve sightlines and manoeuvrability; occasional fires and building activity did the rest to reduce the original woodland by half. By the mid-1980s much of the area was reduced to boggy, barren fields. Tanks got stuck in the sucking mud, yellow-clay soil washed into streams and lakes, killing fish and other animals as the land deteriorated from constant training.[4]

Finally, the city council took action and launched an ambitious plan to restore the original "battlefield" of thick forests, grassy hills and deep river valleys by reforesting and reseeding the land. The new vegetation helped to control the erosion, and the landscape eventually recovered. In fact, some claim that wild boar and even red deer have returned.[5] Hohenfels is once again surrounded by trees that cover its traitorous terrain. Water sprouts from its rocky hillside and forms two small rivers that flow across the western flats.

Winters are relatively mild in the western area, with little snow. Summers are cool and pleasant. Rain averages about 50 mm a year, propagating a rich and diverse flora and fauna throughout the area. Periodic droughts are common, but the lack of humidity is mitigated by frequent fog that covers the sky due to a weather front that results from the difference in elevation between the lowland districts and the highlands.

The barren and windswept MENA plateau expands in the eastern direction and reaches far into the desert landscape of the wilderness. The eastern cityscape is dominated by two mountain peaks that rise 950 m above

3 *Daniel J. Calder,* **Iraqi Village on Irwin,** *army.mil publications, 31.03.2008.*

4 *GlobalSecurity.org,* **Hohenfels Training Area (HTA). US Army Garrison – Hohenfels Germany,** *www.globalsecurity.org/military/facility/hohenfels.htm, last visit: 23.04.2018.*

5 *Kate Connolly* **No lederhosen, we're Afghans,** *The Guardian, 08.04.2007.*

Western districts located in the fertile greenbelt area. From left to right: Copehill Down and Marnehuizen.

sea level. The southern mountain crest is flat and densely populated. Wadi al-Sahara is the largest but not the most amicable of the city districts on the plateau. The area, also known as Twentynine Palms is not dominated by palms but by spiky Joshua trees, which grant no shade from the blazing sun. The large, central Wadi in the area remains dry throughout the year. Water supplies must be brought in weekly and, at this altitude, summer is dominated by heat. Low humidity and high temperatures draw moisture from the nearby sea and create volatile weather conditions known as the MENA monsoon.

The stark contrast between the eastern highland and the pastures in the west is mirrored by pronounced cultural, ethnic and religious differences within the local population. Only a handful of steep, winding roads link the two parts of the city, a functioning municipal transport system does not exist. The flow and exchange between east and west is thus severely limited, making collaborations and cultural exchanges between the city dwellers uncommon. Some of the eastern neighbourhoods are not even connected to the principal roads. The isolation of these communities creates logistical and infrastructural problems, but warrants autonomy in self-governance issues which, in turn, foments diversity and local customs.

The city's west is homeland to the NATO forces.[6] A third of the population lives in this sizeable greenbelt area which covers more than 5.5 million m^2 of the municipal terrain. Living conditions are better than in the east. The urban spatial structure yields a comfortable ratio of 334 m^2 of city space per person. The area is well interconnected with a car-friendly network of paved streets, spacious car parks and numerous bridges. There are even plans for the construction of a city railway network – most train stations in the area are already built and ready to operate when the connecting train tracks are laid.

The eastern part of town is MENA territory, where the majority of the Muslim community lives and work.[7] The rugged, barren landscape extends over an area of a little more than 3.5 million m^2, which makes it considerably smaller than its western counterpart while supporting a majority, almost two thirds of the city's population. Up here, life is far more cramped as the ratio of living space in the MENA district amounts to a meagre 107 m^2 of city space per person, less than a third of that afforded to their NATO counterparts.[8] To make things worse, its quality and services are

6 ***North Atlantic Treaty Organization or NATO*** *is an intergovernmental military alliance.*

7 **MENA,** *acronym used by the military for Middle East North Africa.*

8 *territory ÷ person.*

Eastern highland districts in the parched MENA plateau. From left to right: Baladia and Medina Jabal.

considerably inferior to the western part of town. On the plateau, only half the roads are paved and are regularly covered by sand. Traffic is slow and driving tiresome; it is easy to get lost or stuck in the sand. Donkeys and the occasional bus relieve the bad connectivity within the MENA district. A brand-new artery road connects the city's eastern border with the airport, but skirts the densely populated areas without connecting them.

Toponymy

Place-names always adjust and change with time, rulers, territories, ethnic differences or colonial power exchange. Names in Combat City change at remarkable speed; no place-name outlasts the duration of the war for which the troops rehearse. As one conflict abates and another opens up, place-names in the city adapt to the specifics of new battlefields. War capriciously imposes its own time frame on the use of names, so that they expire once the battle ends. The correlation between war and name is only one of the dualities that make Combat City uniquely complex in toponymical terms. Everything about Combat City is ambiguous: each image mirrored; every meaning reflected and multiplied in the simulation of the other. Original and copy merge into an urban reality that revokes the notion of origin and defies the specifics of place.

The original name of the town does not survive its counterfeit reproduction. Shadow cities are renamed when their construction is done. Invented names that relate to a battle narrative (or that barely resemble the phonetics of the enemy language) are popular. Baghdad's copy, for instance, is now called Medina Jabal and the rural imitation of Helmand, Iraq is reborn as Ishmara.[9] Phonetical likeness and topographical reality are not always congruent. The districts of Wadi al-Sahara and Nisr min Al-Bahar (freely invented names) are meant to be located somewhere in Iraq, while Aghjabadi (the capital city of Azerbaijan) has been moved to Afghanistan for the battle.

Other city districts simulate themselves. While these simulations are not displaced in relation to their original, they often take on a new name. Muscatatuck, for instance, chose the distinguished sounding name Cybertropolis for a messy rubble-field-disaster-zone. Hohenfels, the oldest district in town, has changed its name and geographical location on many occasions. Currently, Hohenfels runs under the new name of Skolkan,[10] a German town that must defend itself against hostile forces from the east. These hostile forces from the east are, not without poetic justice, the precise same forces that Hohenfels defended in an underdeveloped region of the Caucasus when it was cast as the city of Atropia.[11]

9 Julian Gavaghan, ***The mean "Helmand" streets where British troops are trained by Afghan villagers... in NORFOLK***, Daily Mail, 24.01.2011.

10 ***15 Tage auf dem Schlachtfeld***, TAZ, 26.11.2019.

11 Michael Thormann, ***NATO probt Krieg in Deutschland***, RT Deutschland, 27.01.2018.

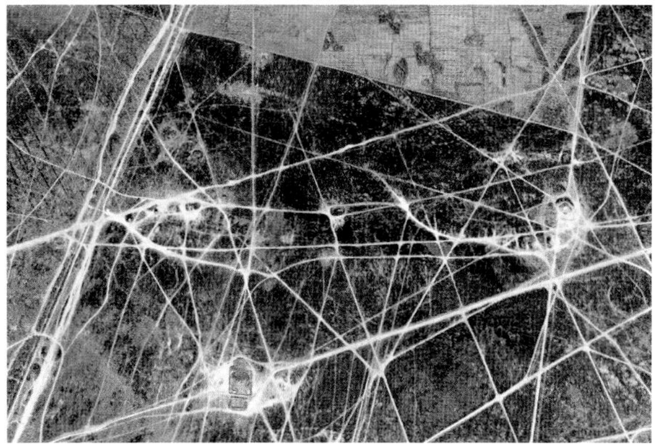

Limits

The city's exclusion zone is used for large-scale assault manoeuvres. The security zone, which is to protect the surrounding settlements from noise, smoke and errant bullets, is riddled with firing ranges, tank tracks and missile craters.

Combat City is zealously guarded; its security belt stretches some 5 km beyond the city's boundaries with an exclusion zone that protects the surrounding settlements from noise, smoke and errant bullets. Meshed wire, warning signs and yellow hazard alerts mark the limits of the safety zone. Soldiers practise large-scale assault manoeuvres with tanks in this area and their deep tracks mark the ground with an intricate network of long crossing lines. Abandoned trenches and craters from missile practises complete the geometrical pattern. The arterial roads that connect the city with its neighbouring towns are also heavily guarded. Access controls avoid having to deal with unofficial sightseers and litigate with unsympathetic press or, even worse, with belligerent conservationists and cultural heritage specialists.

This no man's land is the ideal location for the temporary accommodation of troops (also called forward operating base or FOB), who launch their operations towards the town from here. In its most basic form, a FOB consists of a ring of barbed wire around a position with a fortified entry control point. More advanced FOBs include an assembly of berms, concrete barriers, gates, watchtowers, bunkers and other force protection infrastructure. They are often built from HESCO bastions.[12] These large, ephemeral settlements contain a considerable number of tents that accommodate a command centre, accommodation and a canteen where combat rations are consumed in large quantities. It is not cheap to cool the spirits of the fighting crowd after a long combat day. The water to wash down the bags of processed food is chilled with 2.5 t of ice cubes each year.[13] Despite the intense odour in the communal tents that sleep 150 men each, the level of comfort is far superior to the combat town with its chronic shortage of electricity and water.

The exclusion zone has attracted a considerable and unexpected diversity of wildlife, seldom observed outside its fenced limits. Rare species such as kangaroo rats, leopard frogs and Badwater snails have made the restricted area their home. They avoid the roads and camps and thrive far from human presence. Over time the mammals, amphibians, molluscs and reptiles have learned to associate battle with safety and to disassociate gun fire from being hunted down. Only the birds take to the sky every time they hear a shot.

12 Container filled with earth and stones, used for flood control and military fortifications. It is made of a collapsible wire mesh container and heavy duty fabric liner, and used as a temporary to semi-permanent wall. It has seen considerable use in Iraq and Afghanistan.

13 Jon Michael Connor, ***LRC-Irwin keeps National Training Centre ready for premier training in Mojave Desert,*** *ASC Public Affairs 08.02.2017.*

The most famous and protected animal in the zone is the desert tortoise, which has inhabited the area for millions of years. These reptiles are very territorial and spend 95 % of their time underground. They emerge to eat, mate and fight on numerous occasions. But when they surface, all hostilities must cease. The army honours the tortoise's endangered species protection status and ensures the reptiles' safety at any cost. Unpredicted encounters with tortoises have been shown to greatly alter battle scripts, create confusion about the enemy and cause disastrous defeats. To avoid further trouble, the authorities decided to relocate the tortoises far from the battlefield. No cost was spared to avoid bad press or criticism. The first and largest military-sponsored tortoise airlift in history lasted an entire fortnight and accomplished the evacuation of some 1,100 desert tortoises from the battlegrounds.[14] Their release into the new habitat was traumatic. Homeless and confused, they were packed into plastic containers, flown out into the wilderness and stuck under a ragged bush. There are no reports of how many survived the relocation. A newly erected 120 km, high-tech fence prevents any surviving homesick tortoise from returning.

The exclusion zone has attracted a considerable diversity of wildlife. Unpredicted encounters with tortoises have been shown to be detrimental to battle missions. The military-sponsored tortoise airlift in 2017 accomplished the evacuation of some 1,100 desert tortoises from the battlegrounds.

The desert tortoise is only one of the many encroachment issues that worry the city administration. Encroachment refers to outside interference that is the cumulative result of any and all external influences that may inhibit or jeopardise military training. Matters of dispute are diverse and numerous. In terms of animals, the militaries' apprehension ranges from a pronounced dislike for threatened species, to the disapproval of grazing cows or irritation with migrating birds, as training operations might have to be reconfigured to respond to changing migration patterns or other rare animal behaviour. Livestock grazing is also frowned upon, as it might contribute to the loss of character of the military facility. Photovoltaic installations feature on the list of undesirable installations, as they create a "lake effect" and attract birds which, in turn, will interfere with military flight areas.[15]

Concerns about civilians and their activity are even greater. Neighbouring villages are considered to be harmful because they create light pollution, which impairs the function of the army's sensitive night-vision instruments and might diminish the viability of the facilities. Urban development is also feared, as it will invariably increase community complaints about noise, dust and low flying aircrafts. Additionally, it will raise the demand for

14 Gidget Fuentes, ***After Delay, Marines Relocate Desert Tortoise to Make Way for Expanded Training,*** Usni News, 17.04.2017.

15 Ian Dowdy, ***Evaluating Encroachment Pressures on the Military Mission,*** Sonoran Institute.

Public events are organised sporadically to cultivate neighbourly relations with the civilian population. From left to right: musical recital for peace in Schnöggersburg and the Maypole festival in Hohenfels.

groundwater. In the event of a drought, Combat City could quickly become unpopular with those who desire water resources for other purposes.

The list of possible encroachments is as various as the struggle to hold the neighbours at bay without creating a permanent conflict. The city council has launched several initiatives to keep the peace and show goodwill. Throughout battle season, soldiers are encouraged to sign up for voluntary work, wildlife protection or cultural exchange programs to foster strategic relations with the civilian hinterland. The creation of a temporary, bullet-free green corridor, connecting the northern areas with the south, has proven to be a very popular. Fighting in this limited area is interrupted for two months every year to give the adjacent population a chance to visit the military exclusion zone. During this period, shepherds can drive their herds to graze on the central battlefields.[16] The public relations committee organises small walks with cultural attractions throughout the ceasefire; tours include visits to an archaeological site as well as a special church service in Eastmere village.[17] The highlight of the programme is the popular folkloric Maypole festival in Hohenfels, where folk in traditional dress dance around lampposts, minarets and decorated trees.[18]

16 **INSOLITE. Les moutons quittent le camp militaire,** *Journal L'Union, 07.10.2013.*

17 **Heritage group visits STANTA,** *Carbrooke Online, 11.04.2017.*

18 *Paul Böhm,* **Nach 77 Jahren wieder Kirwa,** *Schmidmühlen Mittelbayrische, 26.11.2019.*

Population

The city's housing stock can accommodate up to 50,000 inhabitants.[19] There is, however, no reliable census of how many people currently reside in the town. The majority of the population is transient and will increase or decrease according to the military training schedule. The population is made up of three professionally-related groups: soldiers in training, professional enemies or non-combatant civilians. There is a diversity of origin, culture or income. Each group's role is crucial to the outcome of the battle, but their interests and values are fundamentally incompatible with one another; mutual distrust runs deep. Each component feels that it carries the biggest burden and is wronged or misunderstood by the other. They bicker and fight on the battlefield, without forgetting that they depend on each other to train, be paid and stay alive.

Right: Washing-lines and abandoned toys are a common sight in the city. Women and children are not.

The city is owned, used and run by the armed forces and 255,500 soldiers fight here throughout the year. They move in large groups; the numbers vary according to the task at hand. Big pre-deployment missions often involve entire brigades that total some 2,500 to 5,000 soldiers each. Minor military challenges are handled by battalion size groups that do not surpass 900 men. The city's streets are filled with uniformed soldiers who are ready to engage in battle. Their day begins with a conflict and ends with combat, regardless of the neighbourhood, the weather conditions or the time of day. Each one of the city districts runs their proper combat script with individually customised narratives. Enemy specifics apart, all battle scripts include guerrilla combat, convoy ambushes, IED (improvised explosive device) encounters, and televised beheadings.[20] The repetition is relentless, day after day, without end or mercy.

Since military drills rely heavily on repetition, the curse of having to relive the same conflict every day suits the army far better than the civilian population. The city dwellers suffer from the violent time loop and typically develop depressive-claustrophobic symptoms. Many struggle with having to get out of bed in the morning and face yet another "Groundhog Day".[21] The majority of the dwellers spend as little time as possible in the city, many dream about obtaining permanent leave. Armed conflicts, precarious security, car bombings, kidnappings, suicide attacks and harsh living conditions make the town rather challenging and unattractive to live in. The perpetual shortage of women does not make it any better. The gender ratio of the population is extremely poor, and birth-rates are non-existent. Ephemeral washing-lines with tattered garments are a symbolic reminder of their absence.

19 See chart on page 64.

20 Scott Magelssen, ***Rehearsing the "Warrior Ethos", Theatre Immersion and the Simulation of Theatres of War,*** *Project Muse, March 2009.*

21 ***Groundhog Day,*** *film by Harold Ramis, 1993.*

Inert civilians – like life-size dolls, robots on wheels, stick-figures and pop-up targets – make up the stable city population. From left to right: a group of robotic autonomous moving targets in civilian clothes. Ambush and execution of two mannequin targets.

DISTRICT	DWELLERS	ENEMIES	VISITING CIVILIANS
Hohenfels	*housing capacity for 254*	*permanently stationed 1st Battalion, 4th Infantry Regiment*	*maypole and minaret festival goers*
Muscatatuck	*housing capacity for 5,000*	*special military unit tasked with representing the enemy (OpFor)*	*airsoft players, amateur sport: run through rubble*
Eastmere	*housing capacity for 58*	*special military unit tasked with representing the enemy (OpFor)*	*airsoft players*
Baladia	*housing capacity for 3,852*	*provided from within own ranks*	*no tourists allowed*
Copehill	*housing capacity for 291*	*special military unit tasked with representing the enemy (OpFor)*	*orientation and obstacle races, historical war re-enactment events*
Lejeune	*housing capacity for 1,415*	*provided from within own ranks*	*no tourists allowed*
Marnehuizen	*housing capacity for 210*	*robotic enemy on wheels (RopFor)*	*3,500 scouts gather for an annual camping event*
Yodaville	*housing capacity for 2,004*	*OpFor when required*	*no tourists allowed*
Medina Wasl	*housing capacity for 1,217*	*permanently stationed 11th Armored Cavalry Regiment ("Blackhorse")*	*box tours offered to family and tourists*
Medina Jabal	*housing capacity for 8,841*	*permanently stationed 11th Armored Cavalry Regiment ("Blackhorse")*	*box tours offered to family and tourists*
Wadi al-Sahara	*housing capacity for 15,627*	*OpFor when required*	*box tours offered to family and tourists*
Chinchilla	*housing capacity for 189*	*special military unit tasked with representing the enemy (OpFor)*	*no tourists allowed*
Anaconda	*housing capacity for 178*	*OpFor when required*	*airsoft players*
KASOTC	*housing capacity for 1,630*	*opposing teams in competition*	*stunt training actors, kidnap training for politicions and diplomats, armament fare*
CTZUB	*housing capacity for 1,357*	*no enemy forces*	*no tourists allowed*
Jeoffrécourt	*housing capacity for 2,576*	*special military unit tasked with representing the enemy (Forad)*	*obstacle course "Rue Stic"*
Schnöggersburg	*housing capacity for 5,922*	*OpFor when required*	*occasional concerts*
	Total capacity 50,625		

Civilians on the battlefield (COBs) are embodied by hired actors. From left to right: Role-players in burkas tending a stall. "Culturally authentic" role-players in negotiations with Marines.

ABSENT CIVILIANS	INERT CIVILIANS	ACTING CIVILIANS
washing-lines and children's bicycles	*life-size dolls*	*students and professional role-players*
no visual evidence	*life-size dolls, mannequins*	*professional and "culturally authentic" role-players*
washing-lines and tended patio fields, children's bicycles	*no targets*	*professional and "culturally authentic" role-players*
washing-lines	*pop-up targets*	*no role-players*
washing-lines and children's playground	*no targets*	*no role-players*
washing-lines and children's bicycles	*over 100 automated targets, including 13 moving targets*	*Infantry Integration Intelligence (IIT) and role-players*
bicycle and playground	*life-size dolls*	*no role-players*
no visual evidence	*stick figures with metal structure and cloth*	*no role-players*
washing-lines, children's bicycles and toys	*occasional life-size doll*	*"culturally authentic" role-players and some amputees*
washing-lines and children's bicycles in the old quarter	*occasional cut-out silhouette*	*"culturally authentic" role-players and some amputees*
planned but only few examples of washing-lines and one bicycle	*robotic targets on wheels*	*up to 900 role-players*
no visual evidence	*no targets*	*no role-players*
children's bicycles and toys	*no visual evidence*	*occasionally*
no visual evidence	*life-size dolls, pop-up targets and video projections*	*no role-players*
no visual evidence	*pop-up targets*	*no role-players*
children's playground	*no visual evidence*	*only for disaster training*
children's playground	*no visual evidence*	*no role-players so far*

Dummy Drag. Dummy or buddy drag is a standard means of moving casualties out of danger or to recover the deceased from the battlefield. (Left)

Mannequin hostage rescue mission with plenty of casualties during an airbus seizure event at the 7th annual Warrior Competition in KASOTC. (See central image right)

Life-size dolls, automated civilians on wheels, stick-figures and pop-up targets make up the stable city population. They are the only dwellers that can stoically put up with the violence and permanent crossfire without flinching or other recognisable signs of panic. Their surprising patience and capacity to suffer without complaint is due to their outstanding mechanical resilience. The dolls come in all shapes and sizes; some are more sophisticated than others. The soft, life-size kind have no specific features and are usually clad in neutral black. Their purpose is to be heavy and floppy when being piggy-backed to safety by the training troops. The upmarket dummy version sports a proper head and torso and comes with a full set of clothes to grip onto during the "dummy drag" exercise. A special dummy travel edition, designed for airplane highjacking simulations, includes a flesh-coloured knob for easy handling on the back of the passenger's head.

A large proportion of the inert dummy civilian population is injured. Hard-shelled mannequins are supplied with detailed and realistic wounds. Most of them lie on the street as if in desperate need of help. The basic dummy version will silently wait to be found and endure being moved to a safer place without uttering a sound. Other mannequins groan or bleed if they are not treated with care. Sophisticated, high-end medical dolls will not only bleed, blink and breathe, but additionally produce five different kinds of bowel sounds.[22]

Avatars are very useful for military training, but nothing can beat human interaction. Actors and hired extras make up the gross majority of the cities' living civil population. Role-players are regularly hired to increase human presence on the street. They animate markets and fill the city squares amid explosions and clouds of smoke. The so-called "civilians on the battlefield" (COBs) are prepped to interact "naturally" with the troops – with loud gesticulations in a foreign language – which, more often than not, intimidates and confuses the young trainees. Interacting with troops can be a rather dangerous job. A civilian on the battlefield is a potential enemy and possible target for any soldier. Many have a hard time telling the innocent from the guilty.

There have been changes in the development, sourcing and (relative) sophistication of these role-playing populations. Former training scenarios were basic. Early military attempts to represent the civilian population

22 *Luke Tress,* ***When a dummy screams for help, the IDF's future medics rush in,*** *Times of Israel, 25.08.2016.*

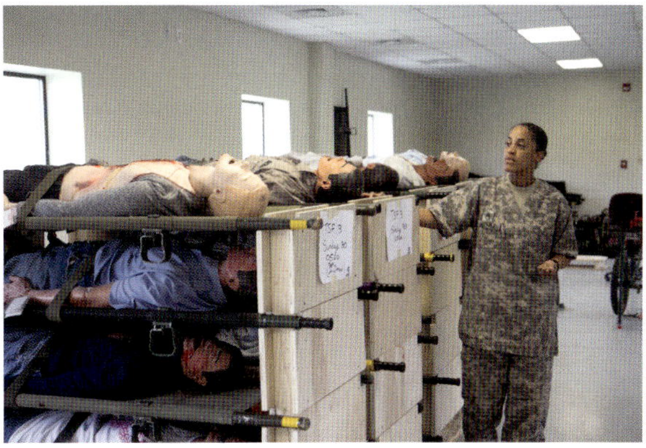

Role-players animate the immense central square of the Wadi al-Sahara district. Local actors pose in elaborate outfits as Afghan civilians on the battlefield in Hohenfels. (From left to right)

did not get beyond a handful of female marines dressed in bedsheets[23] and handing out palm-cards to remind the predominantly male soldiers of their diplomatic skills. Current urban combat training has turned into an elaborate production with hundreds of live-in role-players, who participate in scenarios scripted by specialist theorists. Today, civilian role-players populate the streets that had been reserved for the enemy alone. Their presence adds complexity to the urban battlefield. They might simply linger, wondering what's going on while getting in the way of the soldiers, hold a spontaneous demonstration or peacefully mind their shop.

Their respective roles – as police chief, store keeper, housewife, journalist or aid worker – are part of the greater script[24] that includes peacekeeping and stabilisation scenarios that are integral to the siege. Soldiers are required to engage in cultural transactions with the local citizens while they patrol the streets. The citizens, on the other hand, are instructed to keep careful tallies of promises made by the military and are encouraged to negotiate and claim retribution for their dead. Newscast role-players must write critical battle reports to remind troops that their actions can have far-reaching strategic consequences. Current military doctrine expects soldiers to master the skill of breaching, attacking and killing with cultural awareness and diplomatic skills.

Role-players are hired for continuous three-week periods. Their living conditions are precarious, most facilities have no heating or electricity, water is scarce and sanitation resources limited.[25] The fortunate ones have a bunk bed in a gender segregated house, but most will have to sleep in metal shipping containers or tents. Rules and regulations are tough. No one is allowed to leave the training site for the entire duration of the exercise. For security reasons, phones and laptops are out of bounds. The consumption of alcohol or drugs is strictly prohibited. The military police conduct breathalyser tests on a regular basis and any breach of rules results in instant dismissal.[26]

There are three groups of role-players that work as civilians on the battlefield. The group of amateur actors is made up of students or part-time workers who badly need the income. The second set is made up of professional role-players who work for defence contractors and bring a second language, theatrical skills and an uncontaminated background to the field. The third group of extras are the so-called culturally "authentic"

23 James Der Derian, **Virtuous War,** p. 285, Routledge, 2001.

24 Derek Gregory, **The Rush to the intimate,** Radical Philosophy 150, 2008.

25 Anna Merlan, **It takes a fake military village,** Topic, 28.02.2019.

26 Optronic GmbH, **Civilians on the Battlefield, Terms and working conditions,** https://www.us-statisten.de/en/information/, n.d., last visit: 20.02.2024.

Iraqi role-players teach cultural awareness. Soldiers learn that chewing tobacco or placing their helmet on the ground are disrespectful acts that can spoil an otherwise promising meeting. A marine signals a "culturally authentic" role-player to stay away. (From left to right)

role-players. They are citizens from the enemy country who essentially play themselves.

The daily work routine starts at 5 am; breakfast is served at 6 am and by 7 am, everyone (equipped with Multiple Integrated Laser Engagement Systems or MILES) has to be on the field. From then on and during the entire day, soldiers shoot at them with special training weapons. MILES is a harness in camouflage colour with infrared sensors and a built-in computer. If you get shot, it beeps briefly. You are killed, the beeping stops. An infrared gun is the only means to be revived. When this happens, the computer will affirm the player's new status with a triumphant "Resurrected!"[27] The mission is open-ended and no one can be sure when the official workday will wind up. Actors often complain about having to be in character for 24 hours a day, or that their sleep is frequently interrupted by improvised role-playing scenarios or other unforeseen events.

Realism is a key objective in contemporary military training and there is a growing demand to enrich scenarios beyond symbolic play. Smells of cooking and blood, disjointed scattered limbs,[28] soundtracks of donkeys braying and explosions are orchestrated into hyperrealistic scenes to accelerate the soldier's suspension of disbelief and get him straight into battle mode. Culturally "authentic" role-players, real-life amputees[29] and genuine livestock are considered to be key elements for scenarios that are to leave a lasting impression on the troops.

Regular role-players need on-site support from experts in make-up, culture, special effects, production, linguistics and wardrobe in order to act and look convincing. The logistics and costs involved are considerable and the daily preparation is slow. The "authentic" role-players, on the other hand, will need none of the preparation; their expert knowledge is natural and enables them to add detail and nuance to their role that go beyond the battle script. Lower costs and increased efficiency are a strong argument for preferential hiring.

The same logic is applied when hiring real-life amputees and war veterans as stand-ins for the wounded and to simulate the effects of suicide bombs. The injuries must be as convincing and gruesome as possible because soldiers must be prepared for the worst. Professional silicon and fake blood make-up will never be as frightening as the already mutilated body of an

27 *15 Tage auf dem Schlachtfeld*, TAZ, 26.11.2019.

28 See Strategic Operations Inc, *Catalog of fake body parts*, https://www.strategic-operations.com/v/vspfiles/downloadables/Body-Parts-Catalog-2020.pdf, 2020, last visit: 20.02.2024.

29 Geoff Manaugh, *In The Box: A Tour Through the Simulated Battlefields of the U.S. National Training Center*, www.bldgblog.com/2013/05/in-the-box-a-tour-through-the-simulated-battlefields-of-the-u-s-national-training-center/, last visit: 30.01.2024.

Local actors in fancy dress barter in an outdoor tyre shop in Hohenfels. (Left)

Mission rehearsal for negotiation and peace talks. Combatants practise conducting bilateral engagements in a cultural context. Diplomatic role-play, like talking to village elders or leaders of the community, is intended to help soldiers become sensitive to cultural issues in the way they dress, behave and raise delicate subjects. (Right)

amputee. And it will take longer to prepare. Special effects make-up artists are highly paid and run a tight schedule. A full body make-up of a wounded soldier is far less time consuming and more convincing if the actor's body is already damaged.

Role-players must follow the instructions of set directors, scenario managers and their assistants. Frictions arise when "authentic" role-players, who tend to know far more about their proper culture than the contractual management team, are forced to accept bad scripts, unsuitable instructions or erroneous casting from a crew that has never left home.[30] Some of these role-players are less worried about obeying ill-informed or politically incorrect orders than about the psychological challenges of simulating being a different self in the country of the "other". They must also determine how to function as an adversary for the former enemy-now-turned-friend and help them to defeat their own country without losing their mind in the process.

The civilians, authentic or not, are far outnumbered by the soldiers in arms. Young, uniformed men dominate the cityscape and are easily recognised in their cumbersome outfits. Every man must carry his personal supplies of arms, ammunition, safety gear, tools, location devices, radio, water and food, in case there is no resupply. A heavy backpack impedes swift or natural movements. Burdened down with gear, soldiers run in a clumsy manner and have difficulties manoeuvring over rubble and other obstacles without taking frequent rests to recover from the exertion. Breaching doors and climbing into windows turns into an arduous physical undertaking; the customary heaving and pushing of fellow soldiers through openings in walls often turns into an ungainly or ridiculous spectacle.

The military dresscode makes up for the uncoordinated and graceless movement of the troops and provides a visual impression of authority and control. The superiority in man- and firepower makes them the master of the battlefield as soon as the exercise begins. From there on, the narrative of the conflict unfolds with unexpected turns and twists. The soldiers do not control the combat script, nor do they have exact knowledge of the upcoming events. The narrative is purposefully open-ended and will vary according to action taken. Mistakes in assessment and strategy can backfire and complicate the battle. But the soldiers know that however bad the combat, they will prevail in the end. Their victory is granted in the script, notwithstanding collateral damage.

30 Dabareh Vowell, **Military Role Player Effectiveness and Efficiency**, New Mexico Tech, August 2011.

Early morning urban combat drill in Wadi al-Sahara.

The locals consider the troops to be a rather unpleasant bunch since they don't interact with anyone and move in close-knit groups. Soldiers are exclusively reliant on each other for support, comfort, and defence; personal interests are subsumed into group interest for the benefit of greater protection. Ill-humoured and physically tired, they trudge around town in squad size groups. They speak in code, bark orders and act aggressively. Despite, or maybe because of their age, they act as if they owned the place. They break down walls and invade private homes without any word or excuse. They are jumpy from exertion and lack of sleep. Excessive intake of both caffeine and sugar fuels their erratic behaviour. After all, fighting is extremely wearing on both body and mind, especially in cities. Dense urban fabric increases the difficulty of locating the enemy and requires constant alertness in anticipation of enemy fire from multiple directions. Having to take vital decisions with little time and insufficient information produces mental stress. The sense of permanent danger overstimulates the nervous system and produces psychological disorder symptoms such as insomnia, lack of motivation, high anxiety, neuro-emotional stress, fatigue, and hypochondria, all of which are hindering and undesirable on a battlefield.[31]

Soldiers forget that they are not yet engaged in real battle, that they are fighting a simulated war. It rarely takes them longer than 48 hours to submerge themselves in the battle script without harbouring a shadow of doubt. The fine line between reality and fiction blurs as body and mind succumb to the authenticity of the illusion. Genuinely felt fear or rage can cloud the perception and modify the soldiers' operational conduct: many develop authentic battle fatigue. Military careers are known to have found an abrupt end during the training sessions, some for showing excessive fear and others for unnecessarily killing civilians.[32]

No battle can be waged without an enemy. To guarantee combat excellence, the army selects the official enemy from within its own ranks. Generally, a small proportion of the proper training group will represent the opposing forces.[33] OpFor positions within the army are much sought after and some regiments have taken to embodying the enemy almost exclusively. Re-enacting the bad guy has many advantages. It breaks the routine of having to follow orders and offers opportunities for individual initiative. Not having to adhere to any dress code is already reason enough to cross the line and play the game from the other side.

31 **Field Manual No. 3-06.11, Combined Arms Operations in urban terrain, Chapter 1–13,** Headquarters, Department of the Army 28.02.2002.

32 D. Filkins and J. Burns, **Mock Iraqi villages in Mojave prepare troops for battle,** NY Times, 01.05.2006.

33 Geoff Manaugh, op. cit.

Customised robotic moving targets dressed for battle.

Next double page: different members of the heavily-armed robotic insurgency squadron on wheels.

The opposing forces in Combat City are run by a highly trained, if somewhat unruly, local army regiment that knows its way around town. Their privileged knowledge of the local conditions gives them a strategic advantage over the armed forces; their unconventional warfare tactics makes them a dangerous adversary. They work in small, agile groups and don't get a rest until, if all goes according to plan, chaos is properly invoked; or, if things turn out badly, they are shot in the attempt. The only drawback about impersonating the enemy is that the role can stick. Regular soldiers don't like to fight alongside their OpFor colleagues. No one trusts a former enemy, not even a fictional one.[34]

To avoid major disciplinary problems within the troops, the army has recently decided to supplement their enemy contingency with machine-made warriors. Robots, unlike soldiers, don't care much about the contempt of their comrades and happily play the role for which they are programmed. Robotic autonomous moving targets can be bought off the shelf and customised to suit any battle scene.[35] Once they are dressed for the occasion and fitted with a new face and weapon, they are sent into combat to boost the tireless and fierce looking robotic opposing force (ROpFor). Robots are flexible and somewhat opportunistic. They are of singular character and come with a strong motor and an acute sense of independence. They will readily change alliance for a better deal, desert a companion if there is a problem and change their physical appearance to evade being caught. They slip into the role of the enemy in the morning and dress up as a friendly civilian for dinner. The next day might find them acting as protesters in a public order crisis or emulating the role of a perpetrator during live fire. They love the thrill of the unforeseen, and rapidly adapt and modify their behaviour to ensure their survival. Generally, they live alone or in small groups, it is rare to see more than ten of them together in one place. Occasionally you see a couple, but never in a romantic sense. Maybe these robots just share the burden of being a target, but not a common bed. Their personal hygiene is deficient, and it seems as if they care little about their looks. Their faces are stern and pockmarked with projectile marks, their clothes faded and torn. But they do take a lot of beating throughout the day and have to bend over backwards every time they are fatally hit.

34 Lisa Burges, ***Should OpFor soldiers be sent to war,*** *Stars and Stripes, 26.09.2004.*

35 See Marathon Targets' extensive product catalogue of autonomous robotic targets for live fire training.

Q
BA

W G
W A

W H

HALT WHAT IS YOUR NAME?	MEDICAL AID
SIT DOWN	USE THE LATRINE?
DON'T TALK	WALK
NOT PERMITTED	NOW
WATER	YES
STAND UP	NO
YOU WILL BE SEARCHED	FOOD

Language

One of the city's distinguishing features is its surprising richness of languages and cultures. The population is very heterogeneous and transnational. Trainees, actors and civilians from 53 nations stage their battle within the city's metropolitan limits.[36] The overwhelming diversity of the residents is somewhat neutralised by a deep-rooted distrust of "the other", which hinders interchange and leads to the ghettoisation of some of the ethnic groups. Diversity of languages was a divine punishment in the biblical tower of Babel. Communication is also one of the major challenges in Combat City. The population has to litigate with up to 39 different tongues[37], several sign languages and a wide spectrum of incomprehensible army jargon. Conversations between a civilian population comprised of distinct nationalities are enriched with hand signs and drawings when the spoken word fails. Unfortunately, this communication method is not apt for battle purposes. Precise transmission of military instructions is vital for the chain of command when dealing with an emergency situation. Procedures must be understood and orders acted upon without demur. A wrongly interpreted movement or gesture, a frenzied gesticulation in a foreign language or a misread yellow smoke bomb code can spark yet another deadly conflict.

Soldiers are handed personal translation cards to communicate with civilians in their area of operations. They are instructed to speak loudly and clearly at a normal rate and use gestures whenever possible.

Communication with the enemy is a complex issue. Language is vital if you want to strike a deal, negotiate a surrender or simply get directions from your adversary. As recent difficulties in the war theatres of Afghanistan and Iraq revealed, a basic notion of enemy language is indispensable on the battlefield. Language classes are now mandatory in military training. Soldiers are to memorise 14 keywords of enemy language from their personal translation card, as seen above. For sophisticated conversations, troops will be accompanied by interpreters. These will translate the message to the role-playing combatants who, in turn, must pretend to not understand the soldiers.[38] Hand-held voice translators and tablets with hologram capabilities were meant to further improve enemy communication, but had to be discarded as unreliable in battle.

Combat is not an ideal condition for communication with or comprehension of "the other". Troops are trained to be aggressive, fearless and assertive; there is little space for dialogue and exchange with the enemy. In general, compassion is actively discouraged; too much understanding can be counter-productive. An empathetic soldier will not be a good soldier; it is not helpful to sympathise with the enemy or to have moral doubts about the military operation.

36 Soldiers and staff from Afghanistan, Albania, Austria, Belarus, Belgium, Bulgaria, Brunei, Canada, China, Croatia, Czech Republic, Denmark, Estonia, France, Germany, Greece, Hungary, Iceland, India, Iraq, Israel, Italy, Jordan, Kazakhstan, Kenya, Kosovo, Kuwait, Latvia, Lebanon, Lithuania, Luxembourg, Mali, Moldova, Montenegro, Netherlands, Nepal, Norway, Oman, Poland, Portugal, Qatar, Romania, Russia, Saudi Arabia, Sudan, Sweden, Slovakia, Slovenia, Spain, Turkey United Kingdom, USA, Ukraine partake in rotation exercises throughout the year (this is an accumulative figure, taking all 17 sites into consideration).

37 i.e.

38 D. Filkins and J. Burns, **Mock Iraqi villages in Mojave prepare troops for battle,** *NY Times, 01.05.2006.*

Coloured smoke grenades are used as target or landing zone marking devices in Copehill Down.

Next double page: yellow smoke signal in the Wadi al-Sahara District is used as a screening device to disguise soldiers' movements. Some units use smoke grenades as a reliable indicator for wind direction.

The lack of proficiency in enemy language is not the only problem for the troops. They have to overcome serious difficulties in communicating among themselves. Military interoperability between allied forces often fails due to the wrong translation of a specific command or misinterpretation of specific colour code or sign. Smoke signals are a popular communication resource in military sign-language. Wafts of luminous purple, bright yellow and dense green smoke regularly drift over the battlefield, marking enemy positions, battle strategies and fatal hits. Smoke bombs are easy to carry and widely visible. The vivid chromatic range of billowing smoke adds a theatrical element to the otherwise grey and dull battlescape. Unfortunately, smoke signals are as visible to the enemy as they are to fellow soldiers. To avoid informing the adversary, colours and internal codes are assigned and changed every day. This ends up confusing the allied forces as much as the enemy.

Military language is exceptionally inventive. It adapts and produces new vocabulary with every crisis. Dealing with military emergencies requires specific linguistics, be it to save time (acronyms), protect the soldier from an emotional overload (neologisms), boost the moral (euphemisms), glorify the means of combat (sexualism), or to intensify psychological and social unity among the group's members (slang).[39] Code makes it easier to communicate unpleasant news. "We have two flowers and one oleander. We need a thistle" is a less overwhelming message to deliver for an 18-year-old soldier, than having to say: "We have two wounded and one dead. We need a helicopter".

Jargon lessens the harsh impact of a hazardous reality. Studies have shown that masking violence with benign language effectively alters perception. The euphemism of "collateral damage" for "civilian casualties", for instance, is startlingly effective in blunting sentiment for deaths. Soldiers refer to their dead comrades as "T4" and the badly wounded ones as "T1"; they turn "Tom lost his legs" into "Charlie Alpha 6243 is T1" to avoid the emotional pain.[40] Auspicious substitutes, cryptic codes, ciphered messages and abbreviated words render military language incomprehensible to the uninitiated. A practical translation card (page 78) for the civil population could ease difficulties of communication with the troops and help to improve neighbourly relations.

39 *Adele Wilson*, **Military Terminology and the English Language, Department of English,** *University of Toronto 2008.*

40 *Matti Friedman*, **The Peculiar Language of Soldiers,** *The Atlantic, 04.05.2016.*

Alpha Whiskey Romeo – *Allah's Waiting Room: Mosque*

Ali Baba – *Generic term for bad guy*

Angel – *Soldier killed in combat*

Assets – *Weapons*

BAM – *Broad Assed Marine. Derogatory term for a female soldier*

BMO – *Black Moving Object, a woman in a burkha*

Bravo Zulu – *Well done*

CCP – *Casualty collection point*

CHU – *Containerised housing unit*

CHUville – *Base neigbourhood*

Charlie Foxtrot – *Cluster Fuck*

CIU – *Civilian In Uniform*

Charlie Mike – *Continue mission*

Coercive potential – *Military power*

Colateral damage – *Civilian casualties*

FISH and CHIPS – *Fighting in someone's house and causing havoc in people's streets*

FOB – *Forward Operating Base*

GTS – *Google That Shit*

Hardened Building – *A building with sand bags and a roof*

IED – *Improvised explosive device*

K.I.A – *Killed In Action*

Klicks – *Kilometres*

Lima Lima Mic Foxtrot – *Lost Like A Mother Fucker*

MIA – *Missing in action*

MMFD – *Miles and miles of fucking desert*

MRE – *Meal Ready to Eat*

OBE – *Overcome by events*

Oscar Mike – *On the Move*

Pineapple – *Hand grenade*

RCH – *Red Cunt Hair i.e. very small quantity or just a little bit*

RMO – *Coin (Round Metal Object)*

Rock and roll – *Fully automatic fire setting on a weapon*

ROE – *Rules of Engagement*

Sheep – *Civilians*

Soften up – *Bomb in preparation for ground attack*

Tango – *Target*

TIC – *Troops in contact, i.e. battle*

UXO – *Was meant to blow up but did not (Unexploded Ordenance)*

Wife – *Soldiers rifle*

WTFO – *"What the fuck, over?" A question often implying disbelief, confusion, or discontent. The only proper response is "What the fuck, out."*

Religion

Combat City is surprisingly devout, considering its martial existence. Religious buildings are numerous; each district boasts a local church and a large selection of mosques. Town planners must have anticipated the acute need for spiritual comfort in this violent, war-torn city. Apostolic devotees (50 % Protestant and 50 % Catholic) account for a third of the population, most others (70 % Sunni and 30 % Shia) turn to an Imam for spiritual guidance.[41] A precise census of religious affiliation is hard to come by; the accountability of believers depends on the conflict narrative of the day. According to the requirement for the combat scene, converts can be readily produced to fit the religious proportions of the enemy population. Sunnis and Shias are often played by Christians or by Muslims of other denominations. Specific prayer rituals and liturgical content are of minor importance. Confessional details are lost in the heat of the battle; a pious attitude and a traditional costume tends to be sufficient to play the part.

Most devotees want access to a space where they can gather for their spiritual ritual. The options in town are plentiful. A series of convertible temples, separate from the specific churches and mosques, accommodate the religious requirements of the battle script. The process of sanctification or reconsecration of these temples is relatively simple. Within a working day, crowning half-moons can be replaced with towering crosses, domes can be added to containers, symbols and signposts exchanged and buildings renamed. Multi-faith centres have also proven useful in this context. The "all-in-one" faith model is based on time-sharing a space of prayer with people of all beliefs. Interfaith buildings are cost efficient, flexible and do not require any change of décor or iconography. The furnishing and ornamentation are purposefully minimal to avoid any representational interference within differing doctrines. They are hybrid structures that combine church, mosque and temple typologies to provide a suitably ambiguous spaces for those who need to fight or pray, regardless of their faith and convictions.

Religious structures are not exempt from war-related death and destruction. Current military doctrine only peripherally addresses the moral and legal issues surrounding the use of culturally significant infrastructure in military operations. According to the Hague Convention for the Protection of Cultural Property in the Event of Armed Conflict of 14 May 1954, religious structures are protected targets and require security and law enforcement protection from looting and pilferage. However, military commanders

41 Scott Magelssen, ***Rehearsing the "Warrior Ethos", Theatre Immersion and the Simulation of Theatres of War,*** *Project Muse, March 2009.*

There is no safe haven in the city. Houses of God are not exempt from war-related death and destruction. Even the dead are not safe. Graveyards, formerly a no-go in combat operations, are now being used as hiding places for warriors and weapons.

Next double page: a colourful collection of the city's mosques.

quickly educate, inform and continually remind the urban populace that the protection of houses of God, as mentioned above, may be waived if they are considered to be a military objective or if there is no feasible alternative to obtain a similar military advantage.

The potential danger of being attacked dampens the soldiers' desire to use the city's temples or churches. They prefer to bring their personal chaplain to cater for their non-scripted spiritual needs. The army chaplain moves with the troops and travels light. His pastoral duties are to nurture the living, care for the wounded and honour the fallen: a titanic task, considering the number of bodies and religious inclinations. Far from the former "building up the indomitable spirit of the army" and prayers for victory over the enemy, chaplains now see their role as one of support and moral guidance for the troops. The chaplain's uniform includes a firearm for good measure.

20

مسجد السنة

Food

Food in Combat City is scanty but strategic. There are six official restaurants, one pizza shop and seven coffee shops in town, but most of them are permanently closed. The "Kamel Dog" café is one of the few that is open and serves snacks on a regular basis. Its owner, Mr Hakim is famous for being the most prolific killer of army trainees. He plays the part of a friendly village hot dog salesman who, once he gains the soldiers' trust, delivers bombs instead of food.[42]

Prop kebabs, hardened beef and a counterfeit sheep animate the city's market. With such a wide range of modified produce on offer, it is easy to mistake authentic sweet potatoes for real hand grenades.

Plenty of butchers, bakers and pushcart venders offer their produce in the city bazaars.[43] The range of street food is ample, but it is hard to digest. Fruit and vegetables are plastic reproductions, meat and sausages are painted on plywood boards. Even bread has an eternal lifespan here. It can be washed under a hose if the layers of accumulated dust become too thick.

The best meals are prepared at home by the role-players who tend to bring their own supplies and cook them on little makeshift stoves positioned outside their humble dwellings. Ingredients, preparation and level of spicing vary according to the ethnic background of the cook. The battle narrative determines the nationality of the actor and, as a consequence, the flavour of the home-made food. The clatter of metal plates, the smell and the sight of authentic dishes are all part of the military immersion plan.

Soldiers do not rely on local supplies for food. They bring their own special combat rations to eat during the battle. Years of alimentary research has produced a wide range of lightweight, long-lasting convenience food that can be easily carried by the soldier and consumed in adverse conditions. MRE or "meals ready to eat" are high-tech food packets for troops in combat. They last forever (ten-year shelf life), fit easily in the soldier's backpack and guarantee a 24-hour supply of the carrier's protein, sugar and caffeine intake. They are provisions to have on the go, providing comfort food far from home and a supply of energy in physically challenging conditions.

The latest version of combat food is called "First Strike Ration" and comes in a brick size thermoplastic bag with 18 sachets of equal colour but different sizes. The sachets, whose list of ingredients offer some clues about the mysterious content, can be freely combined to make up

42 D. Filkins and J. Burns, **Mock Iraqi villages in Mojave prepare troops for battle**, NY Times, 01.05.2006.

43 Anna Merlan, **It takes a fake military village**, Topic.28.02.2019.

تفاح
MW42

الكرامة

One of the few food stalls in the Hohenfels district adapts to the battle script and replaces the standard "sausage and fries" menu with mutton and rice.

three different meals. It is up to the soldier to choose if he wants to start the day with a combination of an apple turnover, smoked turkey nuggets and banana and strawberry milkshake or if he prefers to begin with orange-flavoured water, a bagel with cheese spread and a handful of dehydrated cranberries with a caffeinated chocolate pudding. Dining options are a pork wrap with barbeque sauce or chicken breast with garlic, followed by a mocha dessert bar or an apple-cinnamon energy stick. A pack of chewing gum, with 100 mg of caffeine a bite, keeps the warrior alert throughout the day. A zip-up bag for loose components or rubbish is supplied as well as a box of matches and a tiny folded ration of toilet paper.

A transparent plastic bag with a heater unit offers the option of heating the food. It is designed to be used by combatants at war, but can only be activated if a compatible fire extinguisher is readily available and good ventilation is ensured. According to the instruction manual, the flameless ration heater must never be stored near an open flame, as the vapours released from activated heaters contain hydrogen and flammable gas. Considering the difficulties complying with these requirements on the battlefield, a cold meal might have its advantages.

All battle rations are tightly packed, highly processed and nearly imperishable. There are, however, differences in content, packaging and selection according to provenance of the troop. Men from the north tend to carry crisp bread, dry porridge and small tins of beef or pork in their "Sissi" rations.[44] French troops thrive on a choice of tinned rabbit, lamb, duck, veal or salmon. The German combat ration comes in a simple grey cardboard box with attractive letters. It offers a combination of goulash, spicy sausage, Italian pasta and tofu stir-fry, as well as thinly-sliced rye bread and water purifying tablets. The Greek pack is filled with a variation of commercial supermarket tins. Their special treat is honey and a pack of locally commandeered cigarettes. The Irish food ration is somewhat similar to the British one. Both include sausage and beans, Irish stew and chicken curry. Complementary packets of sanitary foot powder are exclusively supplied to the Irish.

Italian battle rations are colour-coded to help. The menu is comprised of *tortellini al ragù, pasta e fagioli, wurstel, tacchino in gelatina, insalata di riso* and fruit cocktail. A multi-vitamin tablet, toothpick and three small disposable toothbrushes with pre-applied tooth powder are included for aftercare.

44 Sissi (forest bandit) is a Finnish term for light infantry conducting sabotage and guerrilla warfare operations behind enemy lines.

Informal egg market in the periphery of the Wadi al-Sahara district. Open-air markets in the area are considered to be dangerous. To be safe, soldiers send armed robots to do the shopping.

The Israeli food box is bigger than its counterparts and has to be shared between soldiers. Rice-filled vine leaves, tuna, olives, and pickled cucumbers come in cans. Even chocolate and peanuts are tinned. There is no fireless heater provided in the Israeli battle ration; most soldiers heat their food by burning toilet paper soaked in tuna oil.

There is a flourishing exchange market for combat food rations for those who need a change of menu and have time to pop down to the centre of town. Soldiers who partake in multinational operations can swap food rations directly during night guard. Some of the practical, outdoor types prefer to go hunting to add fresh protein to their processed food. The added value, nutrients aside, is their comrades' admiration for the lucky hunter who returns with prey.

Economy

The city of eternal conflict is built around military operations and feeds off its booming industry. All activity in the city is related to the continuous creation and consumption of custom-made conflicts of all types and sizes. A steady stream of investments from armament corporations, government funds and military budgets drive the economic motor of the city, and 95 % of the employment is generated by the armed forces. The remaining 5 % of employment is sustained by the gaming and entertainment industry. Many of Hollywood's set makers and special effects specialists, who were formerly hired to build elaborate sets for the perfect battle scene, have since returned to shoot patriotic war movies, series about the return of servicemen or large feature conservation pieces. While filmmakers now hire parts of the city to shoot films, Hollywood's finest merge digitalised versions of Combat City and urban combat training scenarios directly into the mass market of video games. Other activities like re-enactment battles, airsoft combat, kidnap and survival courses, as well as the occasional wedding reception, prefer to use the city in analogue mode.[45]

The benefits of the battle activity reach far beyond the municipal limits. A little less than half of the economic activity in the surrounding areas is directly related to warfare practice. The largest spending categories in the area are real estate and maintenance contracts. The demand for construction work is high, and new buildings rise with every conflict. Specialists are needed to continuously customise and update existing housing stock. The reconstruction and repairs from combat practice keep contractors busy and ensure steady work for local handymen.

Neighbouring commerce and service industries also benefit from the military spending impact. Dining and drinking venues in Combat City's vicinity are third on the list with 15 % of the armies' spending volume. Electric power generation and accommodation make up 10 % of the total, and the mysterious sounding "intangible assets", such as casino hotels, are quantified at 6 %. Waste management comes last with a scant 2 % of spending impact. Combat activity produces a healthy appetite. Soldiers spent 40 % of their money on food in neighbouring towns. Steakhouses and fast-food places are high on the list. They spend 22 % of their funds in the petrol station, 19 % on general and consumer goods rental, 3 % on groceries and the rest on entertainment, lodging and special services.[46]

45 See **KASOTC catalogue training courses**, www.kasotc.com/training-courses, last visit: 30.01.2024.

46 **Economic Impact Analysis of Atterbury-Muscatatuck, Section 2: Facility Spending Impact**, V600 Capstone Report, Indiana University School of Public and Environmental Affairs, 24.04.2013.

The weekly flea-market in the Hohenfels district offers a wide range of second-hand merchandise; leisure related products like cross country and downhill skis can be found in the travel section.

Some soldiers do voluntary work in their time off. The army is keen to be seen as a responsible neighbour and encourages their servicemen to do some community work. The symbolic impact of the charitable work on the population tends to be greater than the economic one. In proportion, activities like youth mentoring lead the list with up to 17 % of the volunteer time spend, followed by military veteran affairs with a total of 12 %. Poverty relief and religious activities are at an equal 11 %. Other activities include neighbourhood clean-up with 7 %, emergency services with 5 % and animal care with 1.3 %.[47] Nobody talks about killing or guns.

47 *Ibid.*

Ecology

Despite the uplifting tenor of the city's environmental mission statement, which claims that "we hold ourselves to a very high standard of protecting the environment, as well as human health", no one can argue against the fact that environmental damage is tolerated by the military as an unavoidable form of collateral damage.

Combat City's carbon footprint is enormous. The logistics of getting the troops in and out of town are far more contaminating than the actual exercises on site. Most rotations only last a few days; the maximum battle does not exceed a fortnight of fighting. The planning and coordination, on the other hand, requires six months of preparation and relies upon an extensive global network of container ships, trucks, and cargo trains to provide the troops with everything they need. Each rotation unit arrives with its own equipment – they will only fight with their proper gear.[48] The shipping of tanks and ammunition, the haulage of Humvees, the installation of generators and tents, as well as provision of food and water for the entire crowd is a logistical challenge that entails vast sums of money, energy and waste.

As the city has no reliable electric power grid, energy supply is unstable and insufficient even in peaceful times. A massive amount of shipped-in, fuel-driven generators produce electric power for missile, surveillance and weapon systems. Aviation support and earth satellite terminals rely on permanent access to high kilowattage generated by fuel. Air conditioning for tents, buildings, kitchens, water purification and laundry units also need a steady power supply, as do the innumerable phone and game devices that are plugged in at night to be fully charged in time for the next killing game.

The military is the single largest institutional consumer of hydrocarbons in the world. Everything runs on, or is generated with liquid fuel. The pressing affairs of war leave little room to contemplate the benefits of environmental competence. Overproduction of generator made electricity is chronic on the battlefield.[49] Commanders are less concerned with energy efficiency than with a good constant power flow to guarantee the effectiveness of the war machine and assure the soldier's comfort. No one bothers to calculate the non-linear relationship of fuel used versus energy produced. If one considers that it takes several litres of petrol to

48 Geoff Manaugh, op. cit.

49 John Vavrin P.E, **Power and energy considerations at forward operating bases,** Engineer Research and Development Center, US Army corps of Engineers, 16.06.2010.

The Muscatatuck annual disaster exercise accounts for the district's trashy look. Abandoned cars and piles of rubble create an adequate setting for the newly-built "destroyed" structures. Burnt helicopters, shot-up tanks and twisted metal structures are left behind to disintegrate in a picturesque way.

transport one litre of generator fuel to the battle scene, one must assume that a lot of energy is wasted before it can ever be used. Once installed, 50 % of energy is lost in the process of heating or cooling the town's buildings and tents.[50] Non-existent windowpanes, broken doors and gaping hand grenade perforations greatly reduce the energetic efficiency of the buildings, but sustainability is not high on the city's list. First attempts to remedy heat lost and poor isolation have had little success. The enthusiasm for tent foaming, a makeshift technique of spraying the exterior skin of the large tents with layers of chemical foam to improve insulation, has given way to doubt.[51] Apart from creating a visually displeasing result, the hardened foam turns the flexible tent into a rigid structure that cannot be reused or transported after the treatment.

Combat produces a lot of wreckage and waste, most of which must be recovered from the battlefield and processed in an adequate manner. Some debris is easier to dispose of than another. Ammunition casings and bomb fragments can be collected without major problems. Burnt helicopters, shot-up tanks and cars wrecks, on the other hand, are considered to be decorative props and are left behind to disintegrate naturally.

The city's sweep team from the Range Sustainment Branch (RSB) is in charge of the post-battle clear up. It neutralises and destroys discarded ammunition by detonation and clears the debris from the ground. Once the damaged targets are replaced with new ones, the team moves on to fill in bomb craters and re-establish a level ground. Locally contaminated soil is used as landfill material to even out the projectile's traces. As a finishing touch, target roads on missile ranges are sprayed with a black-coloured, soil-stabilising liquid known as "Rhino-Snot".[52]

All expended ammunition must be returned to the processing station by soldiers after a completed mission. Everything made from metal that has been shot at, shot up or blown up is to be recycled. Staff members sort tonnes of wreckage into piles and conduct quality assurance checks. Neatly stacked and inspected, the metal waste awaits official bidders. Recycling staff wear firearms to deter scrappers from the surrounding towns who sneak onto base illegally and collect discharged munitions for clandestine sales.[53]

50 *Ibid.*

51 *Sgt. 1st Class Jeffrey S. Mullett O.* **Spray foam to improve energy efficiency**, *The United States Army, 29.10.2009.*

52 *Daniel Skrobialowski,* **Munitions Response & Range Services, Range Clearance and Target Revitalization at Yodaville Target Area**, *BSG Corporate Newsletter, Spring 2013.*

53 *Lydia Randall,* **"Marines make millions off ammo casings"**, *Marine Corps Times, 16.03.2015.*

Post battle clean-up with a black-coloured, soil-stabilising liquid known as "Rhino-Snot" in downtown Yodaville. (Left)

Portable toilets do not figure in the battle script. Nor is there any mention of human waste disposal system or sludge management in the city's annual report. The final destination of battle liquids from chemical toilets remains unsolved. (Right)

Abundant quantities of hazardous liquids are another by-product of warfare practice. Heavy duty industrial waste like petrol, oil and lubricants tend to soak into the ground. As the city's sewer system is used for combat training, there are no means to collect and treat wastewater of any kind. The mysterious final destination of liquids from the chemical toilets, which service the entire town and its surroundings, remains unsolved.

There is plenty of scope for improvement of ecological matters in the city. Awareness of the environment and preservation issues should be raised far more often within the council proceedings. There is no good reason why Combat City should not have to abide by existing conservation laws. But, then again, warfare training and ecological protection are contradictory conditions. Learning how to kill the enemy is hardly a sustainable issue.

URBANISM AND ARCHITECTURE

It's been close to a century since its founding in the Second World War and Combat City has grown into a town with entirely specific urban and architectural typologies. Architectural elements – such as high-tech ruins, theatre flats, roofless structures, de-gabled buildings, surface tunnels and container hide-outs – make up this unusual city fabric. Its layout is also remarkable. Nothing within the city is where one would expect it to be. It is perfectly possible to find a suburban residential area next to a central square that faces an industrial estate with representative government buildings overlooking a slum. The way to move through the city is also noteworthy. Accessing a building, for instance, is a challenging task. The preferred method is to ascend the external stairs to the top so as to enter the building from the roof. If pressed for time, entering or leaving through a window is another realistic option. Doors are forbidden throughout the entire city (the enemy might be waiting behind them). In contrast, blasting holes in the wall to access adjoining rooms or buildings is not. The preferential use of private rather than public space in combat operations creates another set of singular urban conditions.

A series of drawings document the wealth of the city's unique combat architecture. Each illustration presents a series of architectural designs that share a common context or condition. The drawing of the Ruined City combines small rubble designs, large hydro-mechanical structures, partially damaged homesteads, deconstructed offices and a destroyed multi-storey carpark. Roofless buildings, freestanding façades and paper-thin buildings are some examples of the Staged City illustration. The Vernacular City blends together a great variety of gabled housing models. Container apartments, a cargo hotel and terraced vessels are part of the Recycled City selection. The drawing of the Orientalised City illustrates walled and de-gabled buildings that contribute to the strategic conversion of a vernacular European village into a MENA neighbourhood. The Big City drawing merges towering office buildings with arcaded headquarters, walled governmental offices, security towers and commercial buildings. The assemblage of exemplary buildings in these cityscape drawings are part of an architectural catalogue that captures the range and diversity of building typologies within the city. Small portraits of specific combat building types complete the catalogue of the city's singular simulation buildings.

Fig. 1 Illustration of the city's ruined building typology. The drawing combines the most recurring combat rubble designs in town.

2. Collapsed Housing
The building boasts a dynamic flooring system. Walls and decks can be hydraulically lowered, raised, or flattened to represent different stages of collapse.

3. Destroyed Apartment Block
This multi-storey metal construction with randomly distributed, rubbled cinder block walls is used for disaster relief and special operations training.

1. Toppled Tower
High-rise collapsed, concrete structure featuring multi-angle breaching points used for urban search and rescue.

5. Two-up-two-down Residence
Situational training exercises are conducted in the partially ruined terraced housing made from unfinished concrete block.

4. Rubble Folly
The reinforced concrete single house structure with serrated walls and diamond-shaped sniper windows is used to practise defence or conquering techniques.

6. Bombed Office Cinder
Block construction with simulated bomb damage. The missing walls of the partially ruined public building provide access to the rubbled interior where combat action may take place.

The Ruined City

Ruins are part of war-torn cities. Collapsed buildings, damaged constructions and broken infrastructures transform battered towns in an unpredictable way. Amorphous piles of rubbled buildings create disorder and confusion by modifying the city's topography as well as altering the paths and pattern of movement of its people. Mounds of debris hamper vehicle access, turning streets into precarious footpaths with new, raised vantage points from which to scan the disrupted urban fabric. Where, one might ask, would *The Third Man* be without the piles of rubble in Vienna for Orson Welles, as illegal war profiteer Harry Lime, to slink off over. Chaos, destruction and unpredictable obstacles are essential battlescape elements to practise war. According to English War Studies specialists, soldiers will not fight in empty streets and vacant housing blocks but only amid squalid and bewildering ruins.[1] It is not entirely clear if the representation of destruction in urban combat training is intended to mirror the existing condition of the enemy town; if it anticipates the devastation that will take place once the troops deploy, or if it reproduces the physical results of a battle already fought.

Combat City builds its ruins from scratch. The crumbling walls that comprise the building fabric reveal the purpose-built remnants of a disrupted life. Missing façades and gaping holes expose interiors unprotected by rubbled walls. Limits between inside and outside dissolve and redefine the concept of public and private space. There is something disturbing about the starkly exposed interiors of partially destroyed structures. Currently, a quarter of Combat City lies in ruins. Damaged or wrecked buildings, such as the toppled, lopsided tower (Fig. 1,1) (which may or may not have shifted the floor plates of the building next to it and is itself a mere structural grid) are in high demand as they are a crucial element in the urban combat rubble training programme. In the past, ruins – such as the small freestanding rubble structures that currently plug Combat City's urban gaps – had been easy to come by. The destruction in urban areas caused by both the shelling, conventional bombing and the firebombing of the Second World War generated an infinite supply of ready to use ruins throughout the battle-scarred territory. Post-war reconstruction eradicated most of the rubbled buildings, and there was little left to satisfy the growing demand from the training centres that began to proliferate beyond the World War battlefields. Combat City declared ruins to be a priority urban planning issue and no effort was spared to come up with novel rubble schemes. Wreckage surveys, architectural competitions and

1 *Professor Anthony King,* **Ruining Copehill Down, British Army Review Special Report,** *Urban Operations Vol. 2, p. 156, 2019.*

Small, rubbled single-floor residences in brick (left) and precast concrete.

interdisciplinary discussion groups were held and their findings passed on to a group of technical experts who were to develop the city's new ruin strategy.

Discussions focusing on how to create the ruins grew heated. Some engineers felt ruins were a natural by-product of military training and recommended the wrecking of existing buildings during exercise raids. They emphasised the importance of "learning by destroying" and insisted that authorised rubbling was the best way to equip each member of the infantry with an operative understanding of levelling buildings and gaining entry through partial demolition. Rubble, they argued, was also an efficient means to limit enemy movement in the city, in addition to providing the defender with cover and concealment. Commanders, according to the engineers, need to partially rubble buildings to provide greater protection or create unobstructed fields of fire. If the ceiling of a lower storey room can support the weight of the rubble, engineers often consider collapsing the top floor of a building before the battle starts.

Critics of this rubble-as-you-go approach insisted that a series of intensive training courses would leave the troops with rubble piles only, as new buildings could not be erected for every training rotation. Operational problems arising from rubbling buildings too soon or rubbling too many were also examined. The resulting loss of defensive locations and the destruction of cover, as well as serious interference with planned routes of withdrawal or counterattack, were defined as undesirable consequences. However, the argument that visibly dampened the prevalent rubble enthusiasm, was not of an operational but of a legal nature. One of the experts observed that while the wreckage of single buildings is permitted on a tactical level by martial law, destruction of entire city blocks would require higher level authorisation. As a result, per current military doctrine, planners must work to preserve the urban environment as best as they can and restrain the urge to rubble buildings.[2]

The verdict of the city council's expert planning panel confirmed that building ruins from scratch was a more efficient option than ruining buildings in combat training. Military engineers now face the novel feat of calculating solid and lasting ruins rather than exploiting the material weaknesses of existing structures and planning their destruction. They began experimenting with simple breeze block structures. They designed

2 ***Field Manual No. 3-06.11, Combined Arms Operations in urban terrain,*** *G-10 p. 558, Headquarters, Department of the Army 28.02.2002.*

Partially or completely destroyed family homes made of cinder block.

and erected basic modules of destroyed two-bedroom houses in various configurations. The stepped perimeter walls of these newly developed ruins were modest and rarely surpassed half a storey in height. Despite the unchallenging structural conditions, most of these early ruins incorporated an empty wooden window frame as physical reinforcement and marksmanship target.

With time, the purpose-built ruins grew taller and began to be partially roofed. To offset the structural weakness of tall, crumbling walls and unsupported gables, each ruin was paired with an intact version of itself. The benefits of twinning complete with destroyed buildings was structurally effective. Typologically, the Two-in-One model constituted the ruined version of a basic terraced housing unit that could be combined to suit specific training requirements. The double version (complete-destroyed-destroyed-complete) of the Two-in-One model is popular with the troops as it offers a wider range of enclosed and partially open spaces that facilitated more complex training sequences. The terraced Two-Up-Two-Down (Fig. 1,5) assembly has established itself as one of the cities' dominant dwelling ruins.

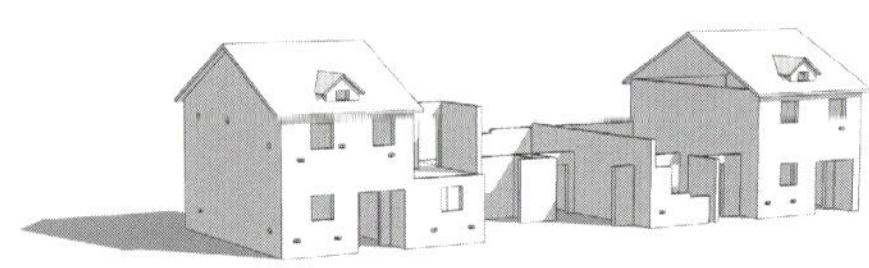

Here in Combat City, constructing ruins has become common procedure, with some remarkable results. The newly built battlespace comprises a large variety of ruin typology, as illustrated in the drawing. Precast concrete follies with diamond-shaped windows and shatterproof lighting fixtures (Fig. 1,4) have replaced some of the rubbled, roofless sheds. A partially destroyed church with its spire standing (top left of Fig. 1) overlooks a three-storey tenant blocks with its diagonally deconstructed façade. The missing walls of the ruined dwelling provide lateral access to the rubbled interior where combat action may take place. Partially destroyed public buildings and damaged office blocks are crafted in what can only be called the "distressed" appearance fashionable in postmodern architecture. The exterior walls of these buildings (Fig. 1,6) are unevenly extended to evoke partial destruction – the Indeterminate Façade project for BEST springs to mind – complete with gaping corner notches and brick and masonry piles.[3] The bare steel structure with rubbled cinder block walls randomly distributed throughout its volume is a collapsed apartment building (Fig. 1,3). This multi-storey metal construction is the first of a succession of sizeable steel ruins that occupy the disaster training area of the Muscatatuck district.

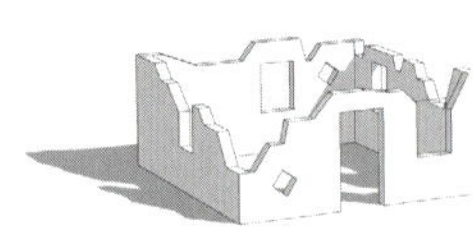

3 SITE's (Sculpture in the Environment) *"Indeterminate Façade project" for Best store,* Houston 1975.

Distressed administrative and crumpled office buildings made of cinder block. The latter (right) has a concrete structure and adapts its shape to the type of programmed collapse.

The integration of hydraulic systems and automation techniques has revolutionised the construction of pre-damaged buildings and has paved the way for a new generation of sophisticated high-tech ruins. These realistic, state-of-the-art, multi-storey collapsed structures have dynamic flooring systems that can be lowered, raised, or flattened to represent different stages of collapse (see image above). Two of the half-clad concrete tructures with sloping floors that surround the toppled tower in the drawing are adjustable hydro-mechanical ruins (Fig. 1,2). Within each collapsed structure, breaching and breaking can be conducted on any type of rubble. Sacrifice panels are strategically placed throughout the city-block sized buildings, allowing them to be breached – creating pathways and access points to trapped victims and spatial voids. These collapsed structures, according to the supplier, contain sufficient rubble and debris to create impressive real "live piles".[4]

4 *Multi-purpose Collapsed Structures, Guardian Centers, Campus in Perry, GA.* www.guardiancenters.com.

The Staged City

In warfare, a theatre is understood to be an area in which military events occur. The theatrical metaphor has been used in battle since the times of ancient Greek tragedy or earlier. The military has long incorporated performative nomenclature and used terms like theatre, stage and actors to describe players, location and conditions in an armed conflict. When the army "sets the theatre", it refers to military actions that establish and maintain conditions to seize the initiative and retain freedom of action. The operational area for the conduct of specific military manoeuvres is the "theatre of operations", which, more often than not, is directed by "theatre commands" or a joint lead between different branches of the military. The simulated enemy towns are the stage for pre-deployment combat training commonly known as "theatre immersion". This two-week round-the-clock military performance is designed to battle-proof soldiers and build combat-ready formations to successfully act in the authentic theatre of war. Theatre itself is a collaborative form of performing art that uses live performers to present the experience of a real or imagined event.

Fig. 2 Illustration of the city's incomplete building types. The drawing combines the most noteworthy stage props, roofless buildings and partial structures the town has to offer.

Combat City is an extensive multiple-stage theatre, made up of countless training scenarios in which different battle exercises are rehearsed over and over again. Staged combat is designed to help make soldiers work efficiently and to fire accurately amid the noise and confusion of battle. Training scenarios, like conventional theatrical productions, use directors, playwrights, set designers, sound specialists and special effects experts to ensure performative excellence and training value. Live fire training, blood and explosions amid simulated streets, make-believe buildings and fake mosques help to prepare troops for the shock and noise of combat. Mastering the manoeuvre choreography by routine repetition is important but not sufficient to prepare the soldier for the genuine theatre of war. Battle inoculation or mental control of fear, combat stress and successful chaos management are essential skills that must be acquired prior to deployment.

The carefully arranged ensemble of purpose-built structures create the stage on which war is to be enacted. The belligerent plot develops in an imaginary place of themed props, false storefronts and freestanding building façades. Combat City makes an efficient use of partial buildings and incomplete structures to define its urban space. Roofless buildings, homes without walls and extra narrow tenement blocks are artfully deployed to simulate a convincing cityscape. Stage sets are reductionist in

3. Sniper Hotel
The six-storey arcaded structure, crafted from concrete slabs with breezeblock infill, is set within an enclosed live fire training area.

2. Gunfire Bedsits
The z-shaped, extra-slim wooden structure absorbs real ammunition used for target practice in the three-storey building.

4. Gunpoint Housing Estate
The four-storey, extra-slim wooden structure features covered walkways and continuous balconies for night shooting at close range.

1. Explosive Residence
The freestanding, pre-cast concrete frontages are designed to withstand the strain of frequent explosions during foreign affairs security training.

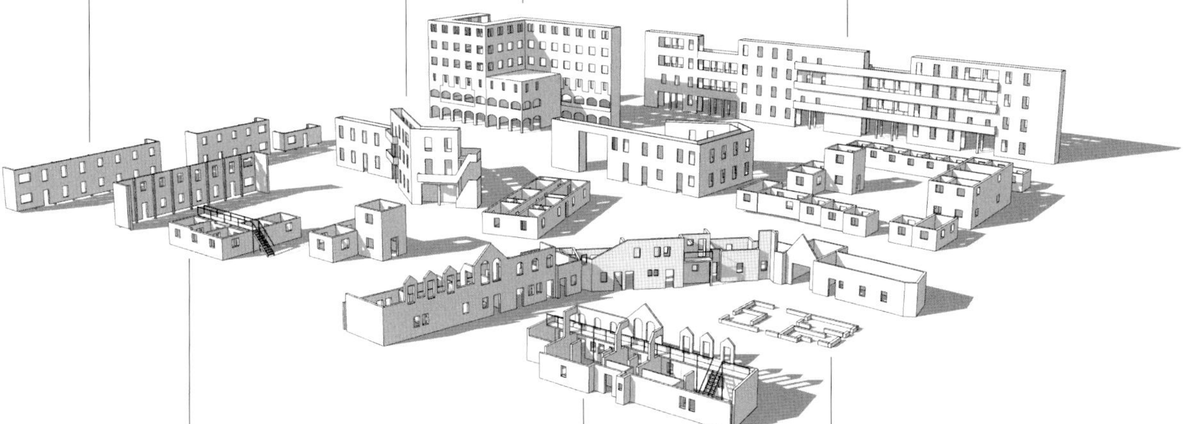

7. Glass House
Assault teams practise attacking a target by using tape, paint, rope or pieces of timber on the floor to indicate the location of walls, doorways and furniture.

5. Kill House
Reinforced concrete and ballistic rubber guarantee the safe absorption of shrapnel fired in this modular roofless structure with upper observation deck.

6. Shoot House
The ground floor shooting quarters of the gabled, cast-concrete structure are used for basic proficiency training.

The French quarter. Explosion Alley. (From left to right)

nature, only those elements that are essential to create the illusion of a city are reproduced for the play. Theatrical props employ the art of visual deception and take advantage of the capacity of our imagination to complete the missing pieces of the picture with just a few visual cues. The curved sequence of gabled residential units with balconies, a covered passageway, a portico and narrow entry doors is no more than a mock frontage (Fig. 2,6). The different shaped windows of the roofless dwellings can be accessed from the ground floor with metal stairs. The surrounding, roofless tenant blocks (see drawing Fig. 2) are simple and less ornate. Their missing tops reveal a series of windowed shooting rooms. A long, narrow corridor connects these practice chambers in the wide, one-storey building in the centre of the image. Stage-craft has been employed to recreate war scenarios ever since the army declared urban combat simulation an essential training aid for the troops. The architectural influence of theatre prop production endures in the city – noteworthy examples are still to be found in its contemporary building typology and construction method.

For example, freestanding building façades, also known as theatre flats, are recurring urban elements in Combat City. Some are surprisingly tall. The arcaded structure of the grand building (Fig. 2,3) at the top of the drawing stands six storeys high. Further to the left, a group of freestanding, concrete façades face each other across the street. The pre-cast frontages which are designed to withstand the strain of frequent explosions, are part of the city's "Explosive Simulation Alley" (Fig. 2,1). The length of the vacant frontage and the frequency of the punched out windows suggest that the dangerous thoroughfare leads through a civil administrative area, presumably close to the centre of town. The tall zigzagging façades of the French quarter on the other hand, mimic peripheral urban environments dominated by high-density housing blocs. These extra-thin structures are four storeys high (see image above). The building with the large portal in the centre right of the illustration folds into the shape of an open courtyard building. Its counterpart, external staircase included, pleats into a Z shape with three dissimilar façades (Fig. 2,2). The largest of the wooden housing blocks (Fig. 2,4) unfolds without a crease. Its linear composition connects three building sections with covered walkways and continuous balconies. The set is not explosion-proof but will absorb live bullets in its wooden building skin. Unlike the concrete flats, the external corridors and stairs of the timber

Glass house dwelling. Residential street with mock-frontage.

structure can be accessed and used as an operational live firing stage. Classic Hollywood-fashion flats can be found amid the larger military urban assemblages. Plywood covered timber frame constructions, generally smaller in scale, depict the built limits of the city's alleyways and squares. The theatrical lining of the urban scene is little more than a thin representative veneer that is propped up by sturdy, boxlike elements that can be stacked and elongated according to the requirement of the script. The hand-crafted texture of the rudimentary support structure has a Constructivist charm and converts the backstage into yet another urban combat set.

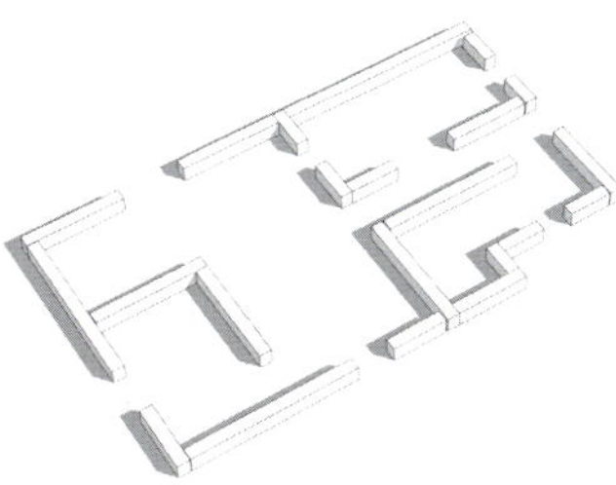

Partial, staged construction is not limited to frontage props. Many of the buildings in town don't have a roof. Some even lack walls. Basic, ground level mock-ups of buildings are rather common in the city, like the one visible in the foreground between the two roofless village structures in the Staged City drawing. Military breaching and clearing techniques are often staged on residential floorplans marked out at full scale on the ground. The so-called glass house drill is an exercise in which an assault team practises attacking a target using tape on the floor to indicate the location of walls, doorways and furniture. These abstract dwellings, which are made from paint, tape, rope or pieces of timber, are closer to a drawing than to a three-dimensional structure (Fig. 2,7). They have a minimalist quality that, albeit unintentional, refers to contemporary stage craft as in Lars von Trier's abstract constructed film set for *Dogville*. Von Trier's film unfolds on a single large stage, empty but for scattered pieces of furniture; the streets and houses of the town are drawn on the floor as if on a blackboard. The actors enter and leave imaginary rooms through imaginary doors, and wander past an imaginary dog and imaginary gooseberry bushes, all outlined on the floor and labelled accordingly. According to von Trier, one of the main challenges in making the film was to see if the plot of a fictional settlement in Colorado could be told on an unfolded map.[5] Both the army and filmmaker seem to share a fascination for mapping out action on floorplan drawings.

With a natural fluidity, the glass house of the Staged City evolved into the fully professional kill house in which the two-dimensional floorplan gains a third dimension by the vertical extrusion of its walls, requiring less spatial imagination from the acting soldier (Fig. 2,5). Kill houses are indoor live ammunition shooting ranges that mimic residential as well as commercial

5 Stig Bjorkman, *Lars von Trier on the highs and lows of making Dogville: It's like a children's nursery, only 20 times worse!"*, The Guardian, 12.01.2004.

and industrial buildings. The repetitive sequence of empty anodyne rooms, connected by a narrow corridor, offer little visual relief.

"To shoot or not to shoot" workouts include room and apartment clearing with hostages, non-combatant targets and enemies. The elevated construction cost of these rudimentary structures does not compensate for their lack of finesse. Reinforced concrete and ballistic rubber guarantee the safe absorption of shrapnel fired from close range. But they do not make for great interior trimmings. There is no compelling reason to cover these robust training structures. A missing roof does not alter the empirical value of the simulation, nor does it modify the path or sequence of the specially-designed obstacle course that unfolds around and within its walls. Discarding the roof is cost effective and facilitates direct training supervision from above. Some buildings have suspended metal walkways that enable instructors to follow the belligerent choreography from above and to adjust the staged environment during training sessions.

Kill house residential development in reinforced concrete and ballistic rubber. (Left) Container Kill house with observation deck. (Right)

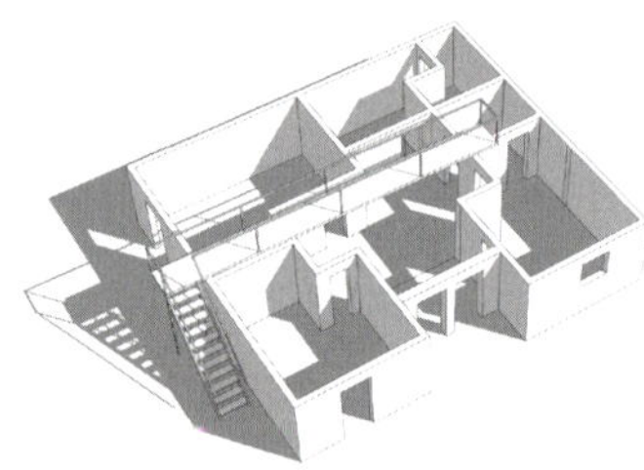

The Vernacular City

Informal clusters of gabled residences, farmsteads and cottages can be found throughout the town. Combat City's pitched-roof housing typology has never lost its appeal, and variations of the detached combat chalet continue to evolve and shape the contemporary cityscape. The latest pitched-roof model is made from prefabricated concrete panels that can be assembled quickly (Fig. 3,5). The cottage, which includes a skylight on the tiled roof and a shatterproof lighting fixture over the entry door, is stockier that its predecessors. The two-storey bungalow – with a steep sloping roof and a large dormer window over the central door – is a suburban type that lines many of the city's residential streets (Fig. 3,4).
An upgraded version sports a 1950s style, recessed, flat-roofed shop extension (Fig. 3,1). A shallower gabled roof admits a greater amount of light to reach the first-floor rooms. It is surprising to find such a high proportion of vernacular buildings in a city dedicated to war and destruction. The archetypal pitched-roof house, basically a romantic or idealised image of pastoral life, seems oddly placed in this hostile urban context. Much of Combat City's architectural heritage can be traced back to its rural beginnings. But why does the pitched-roof building continue to be so popular? Does its archetypal shape and universal symbol of home and protection represent more to the troops than a space to be cleared or blown up? Could it also stand for an imagined, peaceful past or a safer future for either soldier or enemy? Or might there be an unconscious yearning for a pastoral idyll, for grazing cattle rather than exploding bombs? For returning home rather than raiding homes? For peace, even?

The Second World War placed Bavarian vernacular architecture at the core of Combat City. In architectural terms, the planning decision was not deliberate but circumstantial. Hohenfels had been built in the mid-19th century, and its generous pitched-roof vernacular was an architectural ready-made. In the early 20th century, its large, elongated buildings – with their steep pitched roofs, elaborately plastered façades and protruding windowsills – were cleared of their dwellers and enlisted to house combat scenarios for the German Wehrmacht (Fig. 3,2). The outbreak of war prevented the execution of an ambitious extension plan, which would have radically altered the building typology and style of Combat City's historic core. However, the architectural designs for a militarised Hohenfels were lost in battle and the 19th century village was left unaffected. The small, symmetrically placed windows in the village still retain their traditional curtains and painted wooden shutters.

1. Marksman Chalet
The pitched-roof building with a flat roof extension is made from load-bearing clay and concrete brick, respectively. The domestic structure is used to scale, breach or clear.

2. Battle Classic
The elaborately plastered façades and protruding windowsills of the pitched-roof building is an architectural ready-made hailing from the mid-19th century. It is still used for combat rehearsal exercises.

3. Raid Residence
The interior of the red brick building with the sloping roof is filled with stacked sandbags during defensive, inner-wall reinforcement training.

4. Ambush Bungalow
The two-storey bungalow with a steep sloping roof and a large dormer window is clad with plastic shingle sheets which makes the urban roof climbing exercise somewhat unsafe.

5. Assault Cottage
The prefabricated single-family house is made from concrete panels and a red tiled roof. Defensive, offensive and delaying actions can be practised in and around these structures.

6. Combat House
The recessed frontage of the updated, cinder block version of the Battle Classic provides shelter and shooting opportunities for the combatant.

7. Castle House
The concrete structure of the stately home is topped by a flat and a pitched roof to facilitate rappelling training with grappling hooks.

Fig. 3 Illustration of the evolution and transformation of the city's vernacular building style. The drawing combines the most prevalent designs of chalets, bungalows and family homes in town.

Bavarian mid-19th century pitched-roof vernacular. The English take on the German model. (From left to right)

Bavarian pitched-roof architecture gained notoriety after the German defeat in 1945. Military engineers of the Allied Forces declared the picture book vernacular as the official enemy building style and recommended its immediate implementation in the construction of the Eastmere and Copehill Down districts. The romantic image of steep gabled houses acquired much darker tones as many Hohenfels copies were erected to prepare their troops for the worst. Early replicas are quite authentic in terms of proportion and composition. New finishes and materials, on the other hand, are far more modest. Spinoffs, like the stretched multi-family version, located next to the church in the illustration, and the L-shaped row house with exterior stairs (in the centre of the drawing) add building options and provide some typological diversity. Over time and with successive wars, the original architectural style adapted to meet new training demands. It also developed site-specific traits. The staggered succession of the terraced family homes with entrance portals and views of the moat, seen at the centre right of the illustration, is a location-driven, high-end combat real estate option. Most dwellings, like the unsightly, square multi-family unit with two sets of balconies inserted in the sloping roof (Fig. 3,3), are far less glitzy. Combat City's pitched-roof vernacular building style remains in high demand as homeland combat training scenarios are back in vogue.

The gradual evolution of the Bavarian model was driven by a variety of factors. The change from domestic to combat use required a series of architectural transformations to make the housing unit battle proof. Budget and planning concerns called for a cheaper and less elaborate version of the Bavarian gabled house. Building heights were reduced and construction methods simplified. Unfinished cinder block walls replaced the original intricate stucco façades. Finishes became more frugal: the horizontal lines formed by the concrete floor slabs are some of the few decorative elements left on the façade. Attic windows and the odd chimney were only installed for special operations. English army engineers added a new, training-driven feature by introducing a bold, vertical cut in the centre of the traditional country house façade. The recessed frontage was designed to provide shade and shelter for the combatant and enable him to shoot at the enemy without being detected from the street. The vertical recess is interrupted by a square, concrete cantilevered balcony that juts like a springboard from the dark vertical gap. Bent tube railings complete the modernist composition and give the former farmhouse a more contemporary, working-class look.

The addition of an extra "half-storey" at floor level was another major alteration to the original model (Fig. 3,6). The decision to raise the front door 1.5 m off the ground necessitates the use of stairs. The elevation strategy remains an unresolved mystery. There is no written or visual information on the subject. The increased height must respond to some military training issue. Maybe the troops need to learn how to run up and down stairs or receive a new crawling drill at the bottom of the house. The half basement can certainly be used as a hideout from the enemy and for shooting at soldier's ankles during a breaching exercise.

The small openings in the façade enable snipers to shoot from the inside of the building without running the risk of becoming a target.

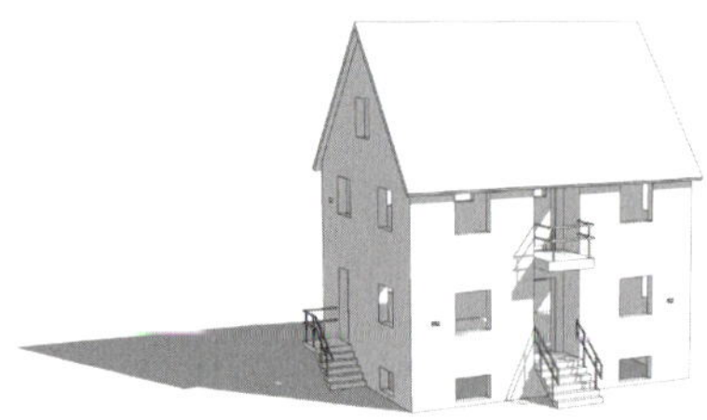

Life in these gabled houses is drafty. None of the fenestration in the original houses has preserved their glass panes; and there is no incentive to replace them. New buildings arrive without them. Metal shutters replace traditional wooden ones. Unfortunately, subsequent exercises verified that any kind of hinged window cover was impractical. Pre- and post-battle lock-up sessions were lengthy and rather tedious. Most buildings are now fitted with galvanised metal sliding shutters that make shooting from – and climbing through – windows a lot easier. The externally fixed rails add a shiny element to the façade and give the buildings a contemporary touch. Shooting does not only happen through windows. It also happens through the building fabric.

Combat City's characteristic "loophole façade" was specifically developed for combat training and can be found in almost all parts of town. The principal function of the small openings in the wall is to enable snipers to shoot from the inside of the building without running the risk of becoming a target. This "loophole façade", not unlike perforated or ventilated façades used in traditional agricultural buildings to guarantee optimum air circulation and keep the harvested crop dry, is formed by an irregular series of brick-size holes that punctuate the building's exterior walls in unsuspected places. Free air circulation in combat architecture is a mere side effect and helps to clear grenade smoke and body odours.

The pitched-roof combat house completed its ultimate transformation during the first decade of the current millennium. During the invasion of Iraq in 2003, Combat City launched a hybrid version to adapt the vernacular homestead to the aesthetics of the new battlefield. The fusion combines a square, flat-roof structure with a domestic pitched-roof building (Fig. 3,7). A large frontal staircase leads up to the residence's

Two different editions of Combat City's Castle House model with French mansard windows, loopholes and defensive castellation.

grand triple entry way. A discreet service entrance on the first floor can be reached by a lateral flight of stairs. The unique blend of defensive castellation, French mansard windows and intermittent embrasures provides the domestic battle building with the stateliness of a small castle. The defensive looking chateau has doubled in size. It has increased the number of doors to be avoided and added the fortified roof terrace as a new battle layer. The figurative fusion of house and castle (my house is my castle) seems strangely predictable in hindsight, given the violent history of Combat City.

The Recycled City

Yodaville was built to be attacked from above. Skilfully stacked shipping containers simulate a fully grown city that unfolds along its radiating star-shaped boulevards, lined with burnt-out cars. The metabolic assemblage of pre-fabricated, self-contained mega dwellings is convincingly urban. Its inauguration in 1999 marked a paradigm shift in Combat City's urban planning approach. The design focus changed from reproducing detailed street-level training scenarios for foot soldiers (street view), to creating urban simulations for airborne operations executed by a fighter pilot (bird's-eye view). A substantial increase in size and extension is fundamental for an urban simulation from above. Aviators need recognisable building patterns, road networks and landmarks to navigate the sky and plot the course of their fire. The ziggurat outline of the Target Tenement Block (Fig. 4,7) is an easily recognisable reference point for a pilot who observes the cityscape from above. The large, screen-like building (Fig. 4,8), is another useful beacon. The structure, crafted from five extra-large vertical container units propped up with a horizontal base, exemplifies the city's growing interest in architectural landmarks that facilitate airborne combat training. The bombing range comprises eight, star-shaped urban sections of differing density and height. Vertical blocks and sizeable structures, simulating high-end representative areas of the city, alternate with dense assemblies of lower buildings and sprawling groups of minor dwellings. The towering housing assemblage (Fig. 4,1) is made up of asymmetrically stacked shipping containers and stands five storeys high. Its geometric composition could be inspired by Kisho Kurokawa's Capsule Tower in Tokyo or Moshe Safdie's multi-storeyed apartment building Habitat 67 in Montreal. Both architects experimented with large stacks of pre-fabricated, self-contained dwellings, long before the military engineers drew up their plans for this target complex. Stepped structures, vertical towers and a deconstructed container building (Fig. 4,6) enrich the vibrant skyline and provide plenty of target points to be hit with rockets, guns and laser guided bombs.

Fig. 4 Illustration of the city's recycled shipping crate architecture. The drawing combines the most remarkable set of container buildings and cluster bomb structures in town.

The urban target complex is made from shipping containers and 23,000 discarded bomb canisters that carried cluster bombs to the Vietnam War. The sturdy five-storey metal tower block with oversized window frames (Fig. 4,3) is one of the few surviving examples of discarded CBU (cluster bomb unit) architecture. The steel tubes, strapped together in sets of nine units, render the recessed façade of the low-tech building with long horizontal shadows crossed by the supporting vertical grid. Cluster bomb

1. Missile Housing Project
The five-storeyed assemblage, made from asymmetrically stacked shipping containers, serves as a target for Hornet and Harrier jets.

2. Urban Hide Out
The private residence comprises two fully furnished storeys and a tower with multiple firing positions for sniper assisted assaults.

3. Cluster Bomb Flats
Basic air support tactics are honed by shooting missiles at the urban structure made from 936 empty cluster bombs units.

4. Connex Hotel
The six-storey container resort provides a rooftop for rope insertion and external stairs to rehearse clearing and breaching techniques.

5. Terraced Shooter Building
The multiple terraces of the stacked container building offer a wide range of sniper training opportunities.

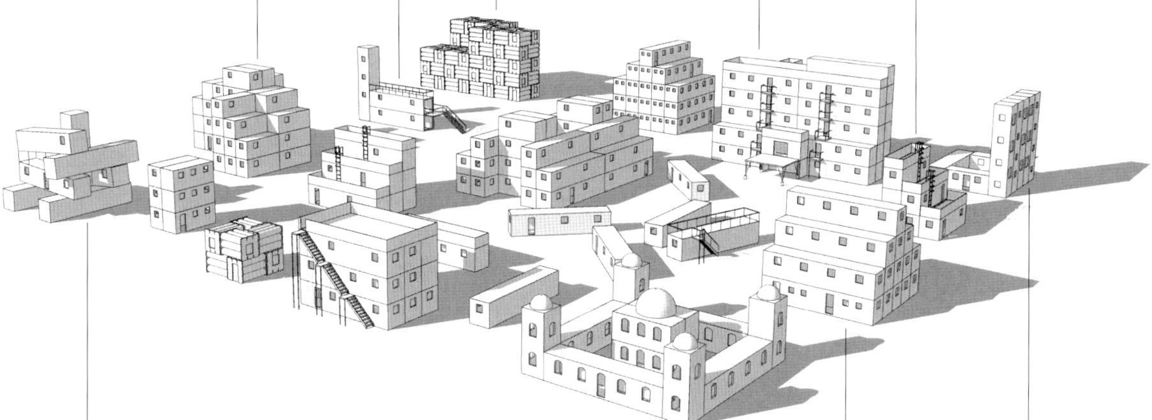

6. Collapsed Residence
Rescue teams use the deconstructed assembly of seven containers with varying inclination for search and extraction training.

7. Target Tenement Block
Once the four-tiered structure is laser marked by a ground air controller, the pilot will drop his laser guided practice bomb on the housing unit.

8. Projectile Tower
The windows in the large vertical façade of the screen-like container building are ideal for fighter pilots' target practice.

Five-storey container hotel with protruding entry portal. Exterior view of the Urban Hide Out model. (From left to right)

buildings used to make up half of the urban bombing site. Relentless shelling has taken a heavy toll on the robust structures which are gradually being replaced with shipping containers. The idea of building the missile range with the very bomb canisters and shipping containers used in previous wars is the military's circular economy operating at its best. The use of discarded shipment containers as targets for bombing practice could well be rated as a "sustainable" warfare training concept. The initiative to create an elaborate ready-made city from leftovers is a pioneering feat of construction that will, in time, modify combat training structures throughout the city. The numeric correlation between shipping vessels, cluster bomb units, ammunition and target practice is enticing but difficult to fathom. There are no official calculations regarding how much ammunition fits into a container and how many containers have been employed to replace and extend the urban target complex. Despite the unknown ratio of bombs to buildings, it seems safe to assume that the live-bombing district will grow by a few containers every time a missile is fired.

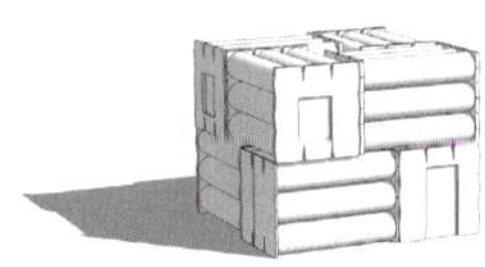

The following decade saw a large increase in container construction throughout the city. New training scenarios like shantytowns, peripheral settlements and temporary structures were quickly assembled with the new industrial ready-made. Savings in construction costs and time stimulated the city's ambitious building plans. Sprawling stacks of identical metal boxes went up to emulate low-income neighbourhoods and walled community clusters. A generic, somewhat impersonal cityscape emerged. There are, however, exceptions to these rules. Creative attempts to provide the standard container with a distinctive flair can be found throughout the expanding town. The distinguished five-storey container hotel in the Muscatatuck district (Fig. 4,4) certainly harbours architectural pretensions. Its protruding entry portal, supported by 1950s-style columns, enriches its volumetric configuration and provides the stacked structure with a distinctive retro charm.

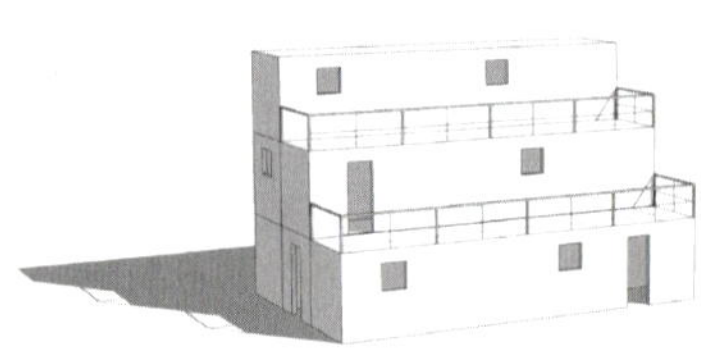

As the city fills up with containers, some standard building formats repeat. The Urban Hide Out and the Terraced Building are two architectural configurations worth noting in this context. The former, for its innovative use of the industrial material; the latter for being the typical representation of urban multiple dwelling in the city. The Terraced Building (Fig. 4,5) seeks to combine urban combat training in a single, compact structure. It provides a rooftop to land on by rope insertion, internal and external

Interior view of an open plan dining area with picture window. Shipping containers clad with military wrap featuring crumbling plaster, graffiti, signboards and ornamental vessels.

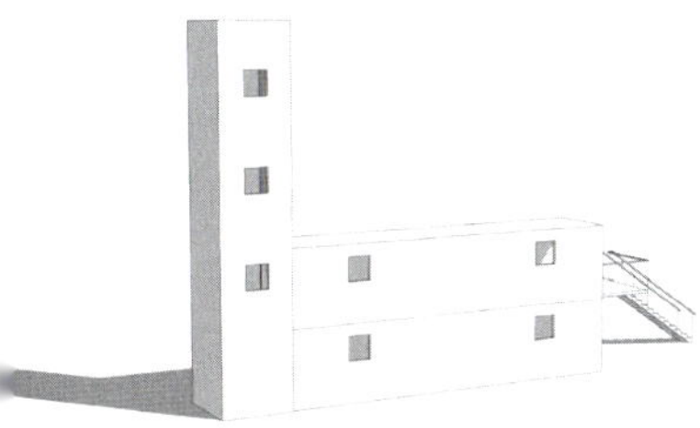

stairs for vertical access, multiple terraces to shoot from and three stacked floors to practise the sequence of clearing a building and breaching doors. The horizontal assembly of these terraced buildings is fast, straight forward and standardised. The vertical use of container-units is more challenging but adds diversity to the regular stack. The playful shape of the Urban Hide Out (Fig. 4,2) is reminiscent of a resting, long-necked creature similar to an ostrich or camel. The vertical look-out tower connects with two furnished horizontal storeys which can be individually accessed from the ground. A third, vertical pipe access is hidden below ground and connects directly to the tower. Furnishings and layout are up to urbanite standards, featuring an open-plan dining area by a picture window as well as a sun-lit study area complete with table, chairs, lampshade and photocopier. Wooden side panels with irregular shaped openings filter the incoming light and provide shooting opportunities without being seen.

The big drawback of using container construction to simulate distant enemy towns is its distinctive corrugated skin. Many construction firms offer faux concrete or brick cladding to achieve more evocative finishes. A cheap way to customise shipping crates is to dress them with military wrap. The design of these architectural garments has progressed from simple camouflage patterns and textures (crumbling plaster revealing bricks below the surface, printed windows and doors) to individually tailored wallpaper (including printed windows, doors, wastepaper baskets and ornamental jars) ostentatiously named "Photo-Immersive Realistic Aid for Training Environments" (P.I.R.A.T.E.). According to its manufacturer, the P.I.R.A.T.E. wrap is a self-adhesive, high performance poly-vinyl laminate with photo-realistic details and site-specific images that allows for accurate re-creation of situational realism for military training scenarios in urban terrain.[6] Its functional merits (resilient to mildew and mould, easy to clean, self-extinguishing and puncture resistant) exceed the visual results by far. Despite rudimentary patterns and saturated colour, military wrap is in vogue. A sharp increase in container couture expands the local combat fashion; many of the simulated buildings are now dressed to kill.

6 ***Photo-Immersive Realistic Aid for Training Environments,*** *Military Wraps Defense Systems, 2013.*

The Orientalised City

The city's Oriental Period (2005–2009), initiated as a consequence of new armed conflicts in Iraq and Afghanistan, was a short but intense five-year period of urban change. Combat City adapted to the new theatre of war in different ways. Some of its districts, like Medina Wasl and Medina Jabal, were built *ex novo* in new mock oriental style. The Dutch, who had just completed Marnehuizen, decided not to modify their brand new district. Camp Lejeune was also hesitant to apply radical changes to the existing quarter and opted for the construction of a new, separate oriental neighbourhood. The Israelis did not have to change anything – their Baladia district already fits the script to perfection. The pastoral village layout and Bavarian building typology of Hohenfels, Eastmere and Copehill Down, on the other hand, requires radical adjustment to suit the new theatres of war. Bold and efficient town planning measures – like the shedding of roof gables, the raising of perimeter walls, the addition of courtyard buildings, the installation of open air markets and the alteration of street patterns – are required to "orientalise" these neighbourhoods. Freestanding minarets, stick-on domes and satellite dishes complete the transformation.

Fig. 5 Illustration of the city's oriental transformation to adapt to new theatres of war. The drawing combines the most remarkable building modifications and town planning measures in the districts of Hohenfels, Eastmere and Copehill Down.

Updated planning guidelines call for the construction of walled compounds, flat-roof buildings and minarets. The implementation of the makeover is complex. Many of the existing buildings need to undergo substantial alterations. Some of the farmhouses are literally de-gabled to fit the script. The conversion process entails the replacement of the buildings' characteristic pitched-roof, visible in the front row of the drawing, with a flat concrete terrace sporting proper handrails to prevent accidental falls and the obligatory satellite dish. Walled community clusters or informal compounds are created within the original village structure by confining individual buildings within its protective enclosure. Some of the buildings are grouped in pairs (Fig. 5,4). The 2 to 3 m-high walls create a "private" space around each homestead which, protected from outside scrutiny, offers additional battle space for enemies to hide and munition to be stashed. The makeover of the farmhouses' community is complemented by erecting a series of new cubic flat-roof buildings in the farmers' back garden (Fig. 5,3). The streets, formerly lined by apple trees and fields are now delimited by a continuous wall with an occasional metal gate. Additional transformation schemes include the occasional placement of ready-made minarets within the farmhouse's walled limits (Fig. 5,6). Minarets are typically built into or sited adjacent to mosques to project the call to prayer. But there are exceptions to this rule.

2. Bridged Residence
High-level walkways between existing housing stock are used to avoid street exposure by raiding squads.

1. Search House
Two-storey plastered masonry structure with multiple rooms, exterior roof access and interior crawlspace for combat training.

3. MENA Accommodation
The walled courtyard buildings, crafted from shipping containers with faux concrete cladding, are used for tactical training with improvised explosive devices.

6. Farmstead with Minaret
New perimeter walls and a freestanding minaret make the farmstead into a protected target which might, depending on the course of action, be converted into a military objective.

4. Walled Community Cluster
The introduction of compound walls and individual watch towers create an additional challenge for street deployment.

5. De-gabled Homestead
The flat roof of the orientalised farmstead is equipped with railings to practise rappelling with grappling hooks. Satellite dishes are added for urban noise.

Walled farmhouses with minaret. Enclosed community clusters. (From left to right)

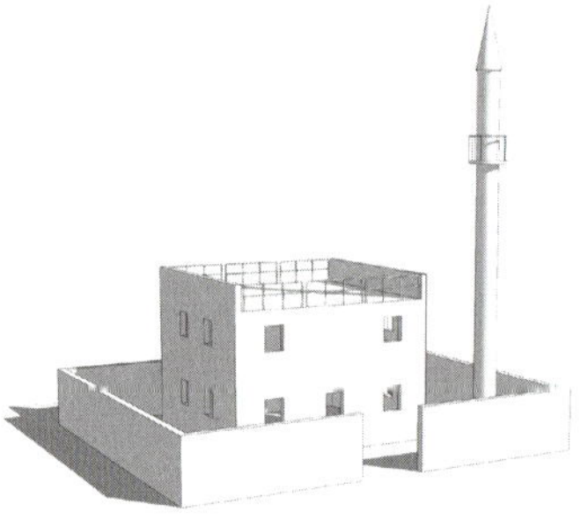

Combat City's Hohenfels district has been a testing ground for alternative placements of these towers. Local authorities developed a cost-effective plan to orientalise the Bavarian village by randomly planting prefabricated minarets next to farmsteads and de-gabled barns. It is now quite common to find solitary, pencil-thin spires disassociated from any house of prayer. The proliferation of detached minarets is matched by an equal number of fortified watchtowers that menacingly peek over the walls of the newly erected courtyards.

Perimeter walls do more than just protect and shield the buildings they contain. They are also meant to be climbed and surmounted. Small groups of soldiers take turns in using their bodies to create makeshift ladders for their comrades, or to heave them across the top of the wall if everything else fails. The lucky ones get to use elevated metal walkways that connect adjacent buildings above the perimeter walls (Fig. 5,2). To accelerate the transformation of the existing building stock, the city council offers a generous renewal programme known as the "free wall deal". After all, walls are a cheap way to modify patterns of movement – altering street activity, modifying access, transforming buildings and creating new visual connections while annulling others. Walls omit visual clues and reference points that assist with the orientation on the street. They are also very effective in altering the urban fabric by creating new, more complex circulation routes. Perimeter walls not only encircle buildings but, if they run parallel to each other, create narrow passageways. They transform previously open areas with unrestricted views into long, dark alleys with limited visuals, few places to hide and less options for escape.

New construction in the rapidly expanding city is required to simulate a Middle Eastern building typology. Most of the *ex novo* districts like Medina Wasl (page 33) and Medina Jabal (page 35) are made from shipping containers. Suppliers rely as much on atmospherics as they do on perimeter walls to meet the orientalising regulations. Container buildings with crumbling plaster cladding and latticed window frames group together in loose assemblages across the desert plain. Some huddle together in a dense, souk-like cluster. A freestanding city gate is the formal entrance to the sprawling container settlement dotted with mosques. Domes in all shades and sizes add a colourful accent to the dusty brown façades of the metal shipping boxes. Some are decorated with stick-on friezes and pointed arched windows. Many of the flat-roof buildings sport individual

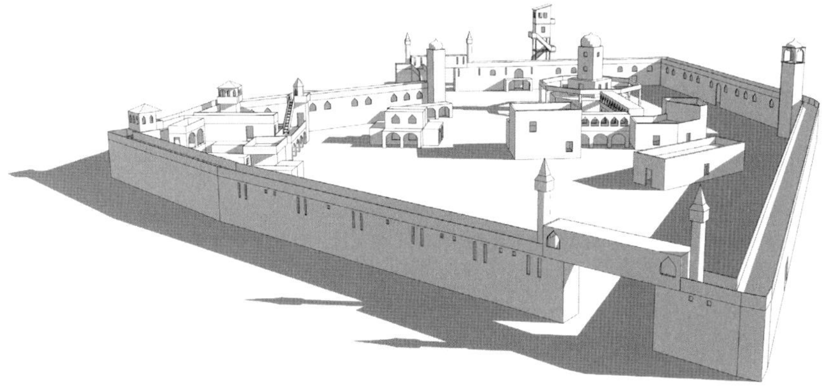

The defensive walls of Anaconda protect a surprisingly ornate town with plenty of oriental details.

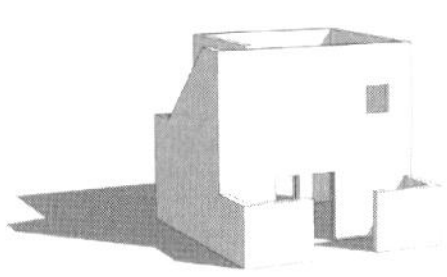

roof-mounted water tanks among hanging wires and wooden utility poles. Palm trees in oversized buckets sway lazily in the wind. Progressively, cinder block buildings pop up amid the prefabricated metal boxes and enrich the architectural pattern of the Middle Eastern neighbourhoods. A growing number of box-like dwellings, complete with walled external stairs, begin to colonise these new settlements. The custom-made Search House comes in one or two-storey sizes. It is a cheap and versatile combat version of simple enemy dwellings within the MENA region (Fig. 5,1). The composition of the humble residence is surprisingly similar to the de-gabled, orientalised version of the Bavarian farmhouse (Fig. 5,5). Both cubic structures are of similar size and incorporate a private walled courtyard with frontal access. Despite its classic design, the lifespan of the oriental housing model is short. Its production will be discontinued as soon as war zones shift and simulations turn more generic.

Anaconda (page 41) is the architectural highlight of the city's Oriental Period. The fortified enclosure, built in 2007, comprises two city gates, six watchtowers, a mosque and a series of arcaded buildings. The entire quarter is crafted from pink painted ship-containers with deeply shaded arches, pointed windows and minaret towers that simulate Afghan conditions. The architectural features of the walled neighbourhood are refreshingly playful and creative. This uncharacteristic love for detail makes Anaconda an exceptional sample of resourceful simulation within the city. Instead of using military wraps or faux cladding to orientalise the fort, the district hired metal craftsmen to customise the shipping vessels with their angle grinders. Every container unit is hand tailored to fit the wartime narrative. Custom-made windows, arches and vertical shooting slits enrich the blind metal façades as well as adding rhythm and depth to the buildings. Golden, onion-shaped, add-on domes provide glamour and deceit. The curving city wall is lined with rows of pointed arch windows that grant views as well as shooting opportunities at the compound. The walled assembly of pink, orientalised containers is the epitome of Combat City's "exotic" period, which embraces cultural awareness programmes as part of deployment preparation and favours combat scenarios with "virtual" travel effects.

The Big City

Fig. 6 Illustration of the expanded, urbanised city. The drawing combines the most significant examples of the town's governmental buildings, office blocks and housing estates.

The city has grown. Stark, rationalist housing blocks dominate the scene. The carefree passion for ornamentation and camouflage has vanished. Imposing new office blocks and administrative buildings line large, modern squares. The city's coming of age is austere and solemn. The three cubes with arcade fronts, visible at the front of the drawing, capture this spirit (Fig. 6, 5). These buildings could have been inspired by Italian formalist architect Aldo Rossi's cube-shaped ossuary in San Cataldo. The prefabricated concrete combat structures echo the haunting quality of the dark, regimented openings of the Italian funeral shell. Beyond the city's sombre mood, size is of critical importance in the expanding town. Inner city buildings stand tall. The high-rise, rationalist tower block (Fig. 6, 1) is an austere, urban landmark that ratifies the city's determination to grow beyond its former limits.

The Oriental Period peters out while troops depart from Iraq and Osama bin Laden is killed. Partial withdrawals from Afghanistan begin around the same time. Neither of the armed conflicts are resolved; insurgency and irregular warfare will drag on for years. The image of the enemy blurs. Informal groups of subversive rebels begin to operate within the protective anonymity of the city. Over the following ten years, Combat City will modify its urban layout and building style to adapt training scenarios for asymmetric warfare and prepare the troops for complex, low intensity operations in large, densely populated areas. Training grounds are extended, high density housing built, representative buildings assembled and headquarters raised. The city is to include office buildings and business blocks as well as industrial estates, power plants, factories and slums. Suburban, exurban, and informal patterns, absent until now, are to become common features of the simulated city.

The newly revised combat manual, *Military Operations on Urban Terrain*, embraces the cities' productive hinterlands as essential training areas within the wider urban spread.[7] All human-made structures that can be related to the city in productive terms (infrastructure, trading estates, factory belt) are to be included in and be part of an expanded, continuous battlefield, renamed as Urban Terrain. According to the Rand Corporation, Urban Terrain is a concentration of structures, facilities, and people that make up the economic and cultural focus of an urban area and its surroundings. The doctrinal definition equates the built environment with population and fuses them into a single, indivisible battle strata wherein

7 *Training circular 90-1: Training for Military Operations on Urban Headquarters,* Department of the Army, 19.05.2008.

1. Tower Block
The concrete, high-rise structure combines the benefits of unimpeded panoramic fire-lines with low risk exposure from the ground.

2. Apartment Building
Platoons occupy and prepare defensive positions within this six-storey concrete structure to control the incoming arterial road.

3. Public Housing
The peripheral housing estate is the site for routine stand-offs between opposing forces in densely inhabited areas.

4. Mixed-Use Development
Marine units rehearse pre-deployment interoperability in the reinforced concrete building with seismic upgrades.

5. Office Block
Practice sessions for kidnapping and ambush techniques with tank reinforcement are held in the arcaded structure on a central square.

6. Government Building
Brigades polish their ability to capture and retain an urban objective in and around the central building and its protective towers.

large numbers of noncombatants (and their interaction with friendly or hostile forces) play a critical role in the outcomes of urban operations. The increased footprint of the simulated city and its dwellers is not limited to its horizontal extension. It also expands vertically. The increase in building heights multiplies interior combat zones in an exponential fashion. Each building acts as a multi-layered battlespace within the city fabric. The combat manual identifies five horizontal battle planes in Urban Terrain. The list, organised in spatially declining order, classifies urban combat strata as airspace, super-surface, intra-surface, surface and sub-surface. This enlarged and dense battleground poses new, complex challenges in urban reconnaissance and warfare techniques for the training forces.

Touring the eastern districts of Wadi al-Sahara, Baladia, Schnöggersburg and Medina Jabal on foot is becoming increasingly challenging. The scale of its buildings, the size of the roads and the distances to be covered in exploring these neighbourhoods is considerable. There are no amenities to break the journey and little comfort for the casual traveller.

Basic notions of urban planning have become an indispensable asset for any soldier fighting in urban terrain. Understanding the structure and strategic value of different areas and buildings within the city can save lives and tilt the battle balance in one's favour. Soldiers must learn how to identify different urban patterns and evaluate their strategic importance within the combat plan. To help with the daunting task, military analyst Lt. Col John W. Burbery and geographer Richard Ellefsen were commissioned to create a military code book that would assist the troops in navigating the urban maze and convert urban complexity into operational shorthand.[8] They worked with the premise that details of individual cities were less important to military command than the overall distribution of built-up areas and the connections that crisscross between them. Their central idea was to reduce the variety of city forms to a collection of repeated and identifiable elements.

The reductive town planning exercise produced a generic city plan with standardised sectors and stereotyped urban elements. *An Infantryman's Guide to Combat in Built-Up Areas*, divides urban areas into six functional zones.[9] A series of 1950s, black and white style drawings help to visualise, but not understand, the nature and characteristics of newly defined zones with unimaginative names like City Core, Commercial Ribbon, Core Periphery, Residential Sprawl, Industrial Area and High-Rise Area. The most outstanding aspect of the military code book is not its zoning scheme but the modular, flexible allocation system of the Urban Terrain model. The relative placement, location and connection of peripheral districts, industrial zones, slums and exurban areas within the urban fabric is entirely free of any planning constraint. According to the new guidelines,

8 *Ersela Kripa and Stephen Mueller,* **Fronts**, *p. 68, applied research + design publishing, 2020.*

9 **FM 90-10-1, An Infantryman's Guide to Combat in Built-Up Areas,** *chapter 2-1, Headquarters, Department of the Army, 12.05.1993.*

exurbs, suburbs, and infrastructural corridors, typically distant from urban cores, can be re-cast as central obstacles of urban combat and combined at will.

There are no rules that prevent placing a suburban housing area next to the embassy quarter with a central square, or combining an industrial district with a school and a hotel by the park. In this new urban order, commercial centres and malls can comfortably nestle next to a prison and a sprawling slum. This laissez-faire town planning style is also patented on a smaller scale. The city's constitutional pieces, its built structures, are freed of their causal connections as well. A mosque, located in the centre of a traffic circle, might well overlook a hotel and a police station with a playground in front of a peripheral warehouse. Other unlikely combinations include a church, a petrol station and a detached graveyard next to a set of walled single-family houses.

The transformation from mock-city to Urban Terrain has had other, wide reaching implications. The face of the city has changed. Combat City shifts from projecting an explicit image of the enemy town to the construction of a nonspecific, all-purpose urban battlefield. The "exotic" flair of the orientalised mock-city is superseded by the sprawling expanse of standardised urban area. As combat training diversifies, the city's architecture itself is progressively standardised. Regional architecture and local details are discarded in favour of nonspecific high-rise urban building blocks like the massive, square housing estate (Fig. 6,2). The prefabricated concrete structure with a central set of recessed balconies is one of the many all-purpose buildings with no relation to a specific location. Current training scenarios are less focused on familiarising the troops with the "exotic" urban environment of the enemy and concentrate instead on collective arms training and urban war tactics within densely built-up areas, wherever the conflict might be. The Big City has turned into a generic urban battlefield.

The implementation of the new military town planning model has changed the city fabric as well as its skyline. Large, multi-storey buildings create urban patterns associated with business or administrative districts. The walled governmental building is one of these sizeable representative structures that define the new cityscape (Fig. 6,6). The plinth of the four-storey rationalist cube sits in the centre of an enclosed courtyard.

Surface tunnels or modular subterranean trainers are hollow, maze-like, interconnected structures that sit above ground.

Six fortified towers mark the corners of the property and define the central entry gate of the estate which is big enough to display a battalion of parading soldiers. The matching peripheral housing estate (Fig. 6,3) with the central arched throughway, located just behind the government building, has a similar urban presence and representative attribute, despite its divergent function and use. The universal and timeless cube returns as a key element in architectural composition. Most new structures are modular, prefabricated, boxlike constructions. Their stark, geometric shapes, like the stepped housing units (Fig. 6,4), are untarnished by details and frills. The only adornment of the flat-roofed structures is the occasional retractable fire escape, which facilitates access to the buildings' windows and hatches. Office blocks, apartment buildings, commercial units and family houses look very much alike. The new building clusters provide urban scale and density but offer little architectural variation. The enlarged city has a distinct rationalist feel. It is austere and strangely monumental in its pursuit of standardised abstraction. A dense maze of occasionally perforated concrete cubes dominate the image of this all-purpose urban battlefield. The geometric shadows cast by numerous pane-less windows affect the architectural composition in an unsettling way. Italian artist, Giorgio de Chirico would have enjoyed the melancholic mood of the new city. His surrealistic paintings made extensive use of long, dark shadows to heighten the theatrical quality of his urban scenes. Some of the atemporal stillness that make his metaphysical paintings so seductive still lingers over the emerging cityscape transformed in Urban Terrain.

Combat City is turning into a multidimensional urban environment with a large amount of novel training opportunities, some occuring below ground. The city's sub-surface, made up of subways, sewers, public utility systems and common cellars is the darkest of the five battle strata it has to offer. A number of large, round hatches, typically located in corners of a square or along a principal street, grant access to the city's subterranean combat layer. The prefabricated concrete gateway to this underworld is 1.8 m wide. The descending shaft is protected by a hinged, metal dome topped by a central air vent. Downward extended stairwells within the core of some of the buildings offer an inconspicuous alternative to access the city's bowels. The scale of the underground network is impressive. A wide and interconnected tunnel system, as seen in the drawing above, invisibly connects the city from below. Special operations use these underground passageways as thoroughfare for dismounted soldiers in their

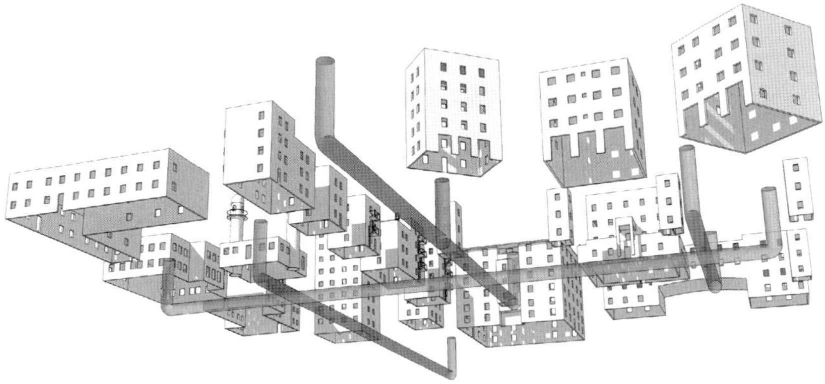

The city's sub-surface, with its subways, sewers, public utility systems and common cellars is the darkest of the five battle strata Combat City has to offer.

quest to outflank the opposition, conduct infiltrations, initiate ambushes and launch counterattacks. The military advantages of travelling undiscovered in the city's subsoil has turned tunnels into hot commodities in the world of urban warfare training. The army is reportedly set to spend half a billion dollars on underground tunnel training in the coming years.[10]

Building tunnels is expensive and time consuming. The prohibitive cost of excavating a vast underground training network spurred the search for less pricey options. An obvious solution is to dispense with digging. Surface tunnels and blind corridors can be an efficient means of simulating the city's sewer system without the use of a spade. Large, meandering structures of interconnected metal pipes and prefabricated concrete tunnel segments begin to appear on city squares and open fields. Despite their airborne condition, surface tunnels stubbornly follow underground rules. The configuration of these maze-like structures is sinuous; corners and sharp turns are unnatural and are to be avoided where possible. According to the training manual, any of these dark and twisting passageways can create the disorientating and claustrophobic sensation of travelling beneath the earth. From the outside, these tunnels are quite enticing. Embedded in the urban landscape, these large, snaking structures conjure up images from land art projects by the artist Michael Heizer, which were created for an entirely different purpose during times of relative peace.

Combat City is well equipped for traffic. It boasts an exceptionally wide network of tank-resistant roads, petrol stations and empty parking lots. Rubble piles and burnt-out cars line the streets. There is a limited assortment of street furniture: chemical toilets, rusty petrol barrels and old tyres. Telephone booths and water hydrants are sparse and far apart. It's a good thing no one needs to make a phone call or put a fire out. The large fleet of broken cars, in different states of mechanical decomposition, is principally used for decorative purposes. Occasionally, car wrecks are employed to create traffic jams or roadblocks to challenge the transit of the armoured divisions. Driving through piles of twisted metal without hitting the brakes must be a thrill-drill for any tank commander. They learn how to never stop. Maintaining mobility is vital to the effectiveness of tanks and crucial to their survival. When stationary, any armoured vehicle becomes a pillbox with limited angles of fire within the city's narrow streets. Driving a tank through a city can be tricky. Combat vehicles were designed to operate in open fields, not in confined urban areas.

10 Matthew Cox, **Army Is Spending Half a Billion to Train Soldiers to Fight Underground,** *https://www.military.com/daily-news/2018/06/24/army-spending-half-billion-train-troops-fight-underground.html, 24.06.2018, last visit: 20.02.2024.*

Their weaponry is not situated for a close-range fight, particularly to the sides and rear where they cannot engage targets. Their main guns are often too long to traverse fully in small alleys, and their limited vision blocks severely restrict target acquisition. Despite mechanical drawbacks in urban terrain, tanks are here to stay. They are considered to be a key ground component of combined-arms warfare and a decisive presence in urban combat. The incorporation of armoured vehicles within the city fabric triggered a sizeable road construction programme that included strengthening foundations and street surfaces to withstand the weight of tanks. Most of these custom-made roads are exceptionally wide. Some span 16 m across. The dimension of these reinforced asphalt strips is as surprising as their sinuously curved path. Combat City's traffic planners favour street patterns with nodes, soft arches and wide junctions. They steer clear of sharp turns and tight curves that could slow down the armoured division, or even bring them to a grinding stop. Paradoxically, the layout of the city's armoured roads is distinctively suburban. Its undulating ribbon network of meandering roads, roundabouts and cul-de-sacs, characteristic for low-density domestic settlements, seems out of place in the urban context.

Driving in town is undemanding. The city has an extensive, custom-made, tank-proof network of roads with reinforced junctions and nodes.

Roundabouts in Combat City are not just traffic friendly but they are also a critical piece of infrastructure for urban warfare practice in addition to their role as a compositional element in urban planning. The proliferation of traffic circles is due to the rise of armoured vehicle traffic with a subsequent increase of roundabout training missions. Tank commanders hone their manoeuvre skills to defend the city's strategic junctions. Combat traffic circles come in different sizes. The largest ones span some 100 m across and can accommodate, in the case of the Medina Jabal, an entire neighbourhood in their centres. The geometric perfection of the circle and the symbolic value of its centre heightens the perceptual importance of the buildings placed within or around it. Most of the traffic nodes encircle a heterogeneous combination of urban structures. The selection criteria for these groups of buildings is intriguing. The assortment typically comprises a public, a commercial and an office typology, as well as a generic tenant block and a walled single family home. The CACTF (Combined Arms Collective Training Facility) catalogue of indispensable Urban Terrain construction, which includes the building types mentioned above, itemises other desirables such as a warehouse, a police station, a prison, a cemetery, a church and/or a mosque, some of the aforementioned in ruins. Hotels, embassies and banks are also suitable, but are not considered to be essential.

Eight arterial roads converge in a large roundabout that connects the southern district of Schnöggersburg with the rest of the city.

Recent expansions in and around the city clearly follow the circular junction trend. The construction of a large, reinforced concrete ring with its radial connections to access roads, blind alleys and service streets is the first piece of infrastructure to be crafted in place. Once the founding circle is laid, any choice of generic urban pieces can be attached to the ring. The concentric city fragment may contain any number of architectural elements. The specifics of the selection and combination of these architectural pieces are not defined in the current military training doctrine. On closer inspection however, a recurring pattern emerges. New circular district nodes contain at least one building related to religion (be it a church, a mosque or a multi-faith centre), one associated with death (a cemetery), another linked to commerce (a business, office or warehouse), to administration (civic or government buildings, an embassy, school or police station) and to accommodation (a housing block or a walled residential unit). There seems to be either a golden rule or an unwritten consensus that mock-cities should include at least one architectural sample related to each of these categories in order to comprehensively simulate urban life. Religious buildings have always had a prominent presence in the city. The numerous houses of faith – colourful and diverse during the Oriental Period – might have lost their sparkle but not their presence within the city fabric. Cemeteries, on the other hand, have only recently made the list of must-haves. Graveyards used to be a no-go in combat operations. Painful setbacks in warfare have seen militia exploiting the taboo or off-limits nature of cemeteries by firing and attacking from mausoleums and using shrines as hiding places for weapons. This has relaxed the former rules and rendered the cemetery an indispensable element in combat training. Commerce has a strong impact on shaping the character of the city's streets through the activity it generates. Shops and storefronts have been part of urban simulations since the beginning. Markets and souks were incorporated into the battlescape during Combat City's Oriental Period. Newly built factories and malls have engrossed the list of commercial simulation as part of the city's expansion plan. Strangely enough, the military never developed a specific architectural typology to mimic commercial buildings. Any size box with an opening and a sign can represent a storefront, a market or a mall. Administrative buildings, on the other hand, are easier to identify. A set of entry stairs and covered porch will provide any large, standardised building with a representational flair and give it that "official" look. For extra importance, a protective wall may be added. Accommodation buildings, as we have seen, are far more

The circular junction, which combines a collection of generic urban components related to religion, death, commerce, administration and accommodation, is the core of a new city fragment in town.

common, varied and abundant in their numbers. Any of the standard models discussed in this guide can be had with or without parameter walls, with pitched roof, flat roof or without either. They come in large or small versions and can be built in good repair or ruined.

The uniting force of the circular shape has the capacity to effortlessly link and combine any of these urban elements. One of the city's new district nodes (see image above) combines the city's latest accommodation model (my home is my castle) with a Protestant church (standard army edition); a walled cemetery with its central crypt; a collapsed container building (Yodaville style); a petrol station; a house in ruins; a walled residential unit, comprising two pitched and two flat-roof buildings; a large government building, complete with an ascending flight of stairs, a matching industrial building; a walled police station with jail; and the entry to an underground tunnel. This rather curious collection of generic urban components comprises the core of this new city fragment. These combat highlights, altered and transformed to maximise battle opportunities, are the essential building blocks of simulated urbanism. The architectural playlist for a basic combat training parkour generally comprises some 16 structures in which the urban warfare choreography of bridging, clearing, attacking and securing can be rehearsed. The simulated battlefield, in this case, is framed by a perfect concrete circle. Could the new district node, which deploys specific principals of urban configuration and living space on its geometric ground plan, be the military version of an ideal city?

Over time, Combat City has shifted from constructing the image of a distant enemy town to embodying a non-specific, all-purpose urban battlefield. It no longer simulates the faraway theatre of war, nor the proper homeland under duress, but pursues the construction and endurance of its own belligerent urban combat narrative. Essentially, Combat City simulates itself. The city has developed its proper rules regarding the composition of its urban fabric, the conventions for cohabitation of its residents, the lifestyle of its dwellers, specific building types and architectural taxonomies, the configuration and nature of its infrastructure as well as the extent and typology of its ruins. Combat City is not a mirror image of the "real" world, but a hyperreal, urban construction in which to practise war. "Simulation is no longer that of a territory, a referential being, or a substance", French philosopher and expert on the simulacra, Baudrillard writes, "it is the generation by models of a real without origins

Construction of Singapore's SAFTI City which will open this year. Air raid and smoke bombs in the central district of Al Hambra in the United Arab Emirates. (From left to right)

or reality: a hyperreal".[11] Concepts like authenticity, fiction and reality are elemental, but not sufficient for the analysis of urban simulacra. The central question about the nature of military mock-cities is less about what they represent than about what they enable. The point, then, is not that these simulations are less "real" than the things they purportedly represent. Rather, they provide spaces through which the violence of war can be generated and performed, and which acquire power through their radical disassociation from any meaningful connection with the real place (or, less commonly, real people) they are said to represent.[12]

Doctrinal conceptions of urban space for military encounters have shaped and transformed Combat City over the years and produced a uniquely terrifying city type that continues to spread throughout the globe. Rotations and combined training programmes make sure that the self-fulfilling prediction of the inevitable city battle never stops. Every year, new, sophisticated shadow cities enlarge the joint exercises training circuit and provide the latest cutting-edge drills. Al Hambra, located on the waterfront of the United Arab Emirates, opened its doors in 2017. Its ever-expanding urban warfare parkour boasts a modern city centre (featured above), a sprawling oil refinery, a harbour, a proper airport and a gas storage plant. In 2020, Snir began operating at an undisclosed location in the Golan Heights in Israel. The massive new urban training base reportedly features advanced simulators, live fire opportunities and underground facilities for anti-tunnel warfare. Singapore's SAFTI City, to be opened in 2024, will supply military forces with high-rise inter-connected buildings and multi-level metro stations (featured above) as well as simulated artillery bombardment for extra thrill. Joint exercises not only hone and share urban warfare expertise and military know-how, but help to develop robust relationships with partner nations while ensuring access to geostrategic bases around the globe. The interconnected network of urban combat simulacra is powerful as a collective. The large-scale implantation of the simulations has constructed, verified and perpetuated the military vision of the city as the new battlefield (a self-fulfilling correlation of cause and effect). The militaristic viewpoint of our urban futures is continuously absorbed, rehearsed and ingrained in these simulations, threatening to project their well-rehearsed violence and destructive force back into the world and shape our cities in its image.

11 Jean Baudrillard, ***Simulacra and Simulation,*** *Ann Arbor, MI: University of Michigan Press, 1994.*

12 Stephen Graham, op. cit., p. 220.

TRAVEL GUIDE

As mentioned in the introduction to this guide, all simulated enemy towns are located on military bases. Site visits are subject to special permissions. Access to the mock-towns can be difficult. In some cases, it might be easier to hire the place as a film set than to visit it for recreational purposes. Press credentials may also prove useful in negotiating admission. Airsoft gaming and battle re-enactment are admission-friendly pastimes that might help to secure an entrance permit. Some of the sites have open days, annual festival for the community, or commercial box tours offering the possibility to sign up with the armed forces. In this case the timing and coordination of a visit is crucial. Be advised that this kind of tourism requires lengthy bureaucratic procedures, flexibility and patience. Travel conditions are challenging, so bring a good pair of boots, a bottle of water, a camera, a notebook and set of earplugs.

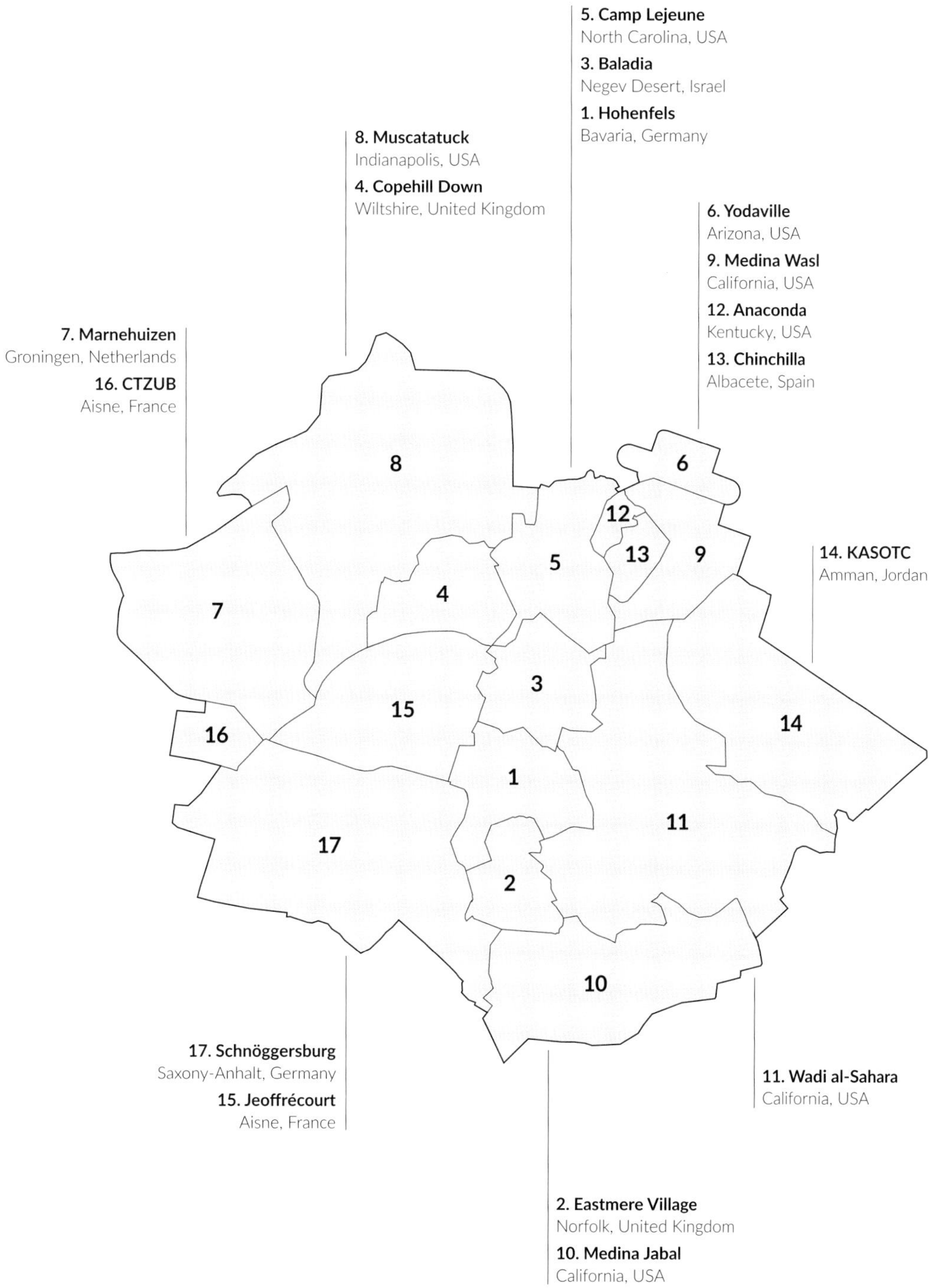
5. Camp Lejeune
North Carolina, USA
3. Baladia
Negev Desert, Israel
1. Hohenfels
Bavaria, Germany
8. Muscatatuck
Indianapolis, USA
4. Copehill Down
Wiltshire, United Kingdom
6. Yodaville
Arizona, USA
9. Medina Wasl
California, USA
12. Anaconda
Kentucky, USA
13. Chinchilla
Albacete, Spain
7. Marnehuizen
Groningen, Netherlands
16. CTZUB
Aisne, France
14. KASOTC
Amman, Jordan
8
6
12
13
9
5
4
7
3
15
16
14
1
11
17
2
10
17. Schnöggersburg
Saxony-Anhalt, Germany
15. Jeoffrécourt
Aisne, France
11. Wadi al-Sahara
California, USA
2. Eastmere Village
Norfolk, United Kingdom
10. Medina Jabal
California, USA

Hohenfels

JMRC Hohenfels Training Area, Gate 5, St 2234
92366 Hohenfels, Bavaria, Germany

Occasional tours are offered during the German-American Maypole Festival in Hohenfels. Ticket booths are located at the airfield parking lot. Special visits can be arranged for press members and civilians through the public affairs office.

Munich International Airport is approximately a one-and-a-half-hour drive from Hohenfels. Leave the airport in the direction of the city. Take the second motorway exit, direction Nürnberg/Berlin. In approximately 25 minutes, the motorway divides. Follow the 93, direction Regensburg. Once you reach Regensburg take motorway 3 towards Nürnberg. After approximately 50 km exit for Parsberg. At the end of the ramp take a right towards Hohenfels. In approximately 12 km you will see a sign for Gate 5.

If you decide to come by train, Parsberg is the closest station to Hohenfels. You can walk or take a taxi to cover the remaining 15 km to Gate 5.

49° 14′ 26.68″ N
11° 54′ 16.17″ E

Restricted Access

Public Affairs office Hohenfels, Bldg. 33
Phone: +49-9472-708-5565

Opening hours:
M – F: 7:30 a.m. to 12 p.m.
& 12:30 to 4 p.m.
Closed US Federal & German Holidays

Eastmere

52° 32′ 20.16″ N
0° 47′ 19.82″ E

Restricted Access

Headquarters DTE E
West Tofts Camp, Thetford,
Norfolk IP26 5EP
+44 01842 855166

Filming:
Tony Burlton
+44 07825 105671
tony.burlton@landmarc.mod.uk

Stanford Training Area, Thetford IP24 1PN,
Norfolk, United Kingdom

Site visits require a special permission from the British Army. The Stanford Training Area offers organised tours during the summer months. Numbers are limited to two coaches a day.

Eastmere Village can be rented as a film location from landmarcsolutions.com.

Eastmere Village can be reached from London by either train or car in 2.5 hours. Trains run from London Kings Cross to Thetford. From there you must take a taxi or walk the remaining 15 km.

If you are driving from London, take the M11 and then the A11 to Thetford. Once you reach Munford roundabout, take the first exit towards A134 for about ten km. At the following roundabout take the third exit towards Swaffham Rd / A1065. Continue on the A1065 for 5 km, then turn right onto the B1108 and right again onto Great Cressingham Rd. Continue straight onto Tottington Rd. Your destination will appear on the left.

Baladia

Tze'elim Army Base, Negev Desert, Israel

Site visits are discouraged and require a special permission from the IDF. Rare exceptions have been granted to press members and artists.

The closest airports to Baladia are Jerusalem International Airport or Ben Gurion Airport in Tel Aviv. Both locations are less than a two-hour drive from Baladia. If you arrive from Jerusalem take Route 1, follow onto Route 3 and then take Route 6. Exit Route 6 onto Route 310. Continue for about 10 km and then turn right onto R25. At the Dor Alon Urim petrol station, turn left and continue on Route 241 to your destination.

You can also travel by bus. Take either the 470 bus from Jerusalem Central Bus Station or the 369 bus from Tel Aviv Central Bus Station to Be'er Sheva. Then take bus 130 from Be'er Sheva Central Station and get off at Tze'elim Camp bus stop.

31° 9′ 50.47″ N,
34° 31′ 56.55″ E

No Access

https://www.idf.il/en/contact-us/

Copehill Down

51° 12′ 24.87″ N
1° 58′ 37.87″ W

Restricted Access

PROW map:
https://wiltscouncil.maps.arcgis.com/apps/webappviewer/index.html?id=43d5a86a545046b2b59fd7dd49d89d22

Filming:
Tony Burlton
+44 07825 105671
tony.burlton@landmarc.mod.uk

Other activities:
Adam Young or Gemma Poolman
+44 07921 199181 or
+44 07884 231791
adam.young@landmarc.mod.uk

Salisbury Plain Military Area, Shrewton Rd, Chitterne, Warminster BA12 0LA, Wiltshire, United Kingdom

Non-combat access to Copehill Down is generally restricted, however permission is granted for certain organised activities, such as field sports, walks and model aircraft flying. The facility has been used for airsoft war gaming and historical re-enactment societies.

Copehill Down can be rented as a film set and for other training and educational activities.

Copehill Down is a two-hour drive from London. Take M4 for about 14 km. Then merge onto M25. At junction 12 exit onto M3 for 50 km. At junction 8 take the exit for the A303. At Longbarrow roundabout, take the third exit onto the A360. Once you pass Tilshead, leave the A360 to your left and continue four km to your destination.

For information on local public transport, call Traveline on 0870 608 2608 (local call rate) or visit: www.traveline.org.uk

Camp Lejeune

Marine Corps Base Camp Lejeune,
818 Holcomb Blvd, Jacksonville, NC 28544, USA

Special group visits are allowed if requesting special permit. Submissions should be made in writing, identifying the name of group, the purpose of the visit, requested dates of the visit, proposed itinerary or sequence of events. Potential VIPs within the group should also be identified. Submissions must be received by the Base Communication Strategy & Operations Office at least 90 days prior to visit. Individual visits will not be granted.

From Raleigh, the State capital, which has an international airport, it is a two-and-a-half-hour drive to Lejeune. Get on I-40 E from Airport Blvd and Aviation Pkwy. Continue for 142 km. At Magnolia, take US 903 for 13 km. Once you reach Kenansville, turn onto State Highway 24 to Jacksonville. Follow Camp Lejeune signs to the main gate. There are other major airports serving the base. The Albert J. Ellis Airport is located about 20 km from the base and Wilmington International Airport is located about 70 km from Camp Lejeune.

Bus transportation is available from Jacksonville.
Call 910-451-5541 for more information.

34° 40′ 3.50″ N
77° 14′ 50.00″ W

No Access

https://www.lejeune.marines.mil/

Requests for group visits:
Commanding General.
Attn: COMMSTRAT. Marine Corps Base
PSC Box 20005. Camp Lejeune,
NC 28542

Scheduling availability:
Base Communication
Strategy & Operations Office
+1 910 451-5655 ext. 1.

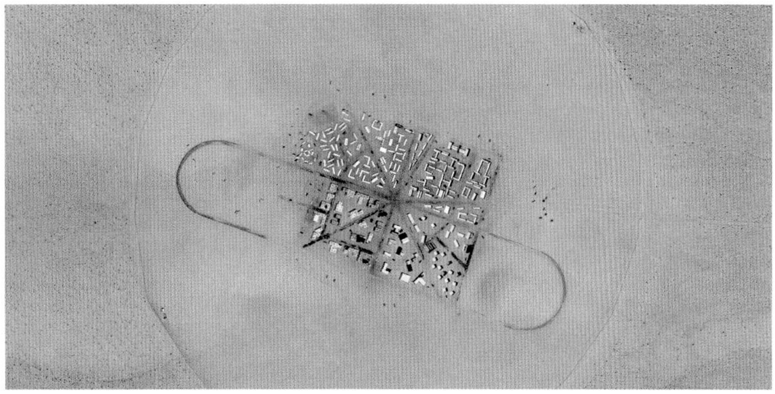

Yodaville

32° 26′ 15.71″ N
114° 19′ 54.20″ W

No Access

Media requests:
Office of Communication MCAS
Yuma_Media@usmc.mil.

MCAS Yuma Range Director
Bill Sellars
+1 928 269-2405
william.sellars@usmc.mil

Range Training Officer MCAS Yuma
Jon Gordon
+1 928 269-6488
john.gordon@usmc.mil

S Avenue 3 E, Yuma, Arizona 85365, USA

A special permit is needed to visit Yodaville. Those interested must send an email including name, contact information as well as the specifics of the request.

Yodaville lies in the middle of Arizona desert and can only be reached by car. If you are coming from San Diego, take the I-8E until Yuma, or alternatively take the I-8W from Phoenix. In Yuma take exit 3 onto S Avenue 3 E for 16 km. Then turn left onto E County 19th St. Follow the road for about 24 km, then turn left for another 3 km and turn right. Your destination will appear right in front of you at the end of the road.

Marnehuizen

Willem Lodewijk van Nassaukazerne & OT Marnewaard,
Strandweg 21, 9974 SM Zoutkamp, Netherlands

Marnehuizen can be visited during assigned open days as well as on Heritage Day. Check the Lauwersmeer National Park for dates.

Marnehuizen is located on the east side of the provincial road N361. It is a 40-minute drive from Groningen by car. You can also use public transport. Take bus 163 in the direction of Lauwersoog from Groningen Hoofdstation and after 14 stops, get off at Lauwersmeer, De Rug.

53° 23′ 10.67″ N
6° 15′ 45.52″ E

Restricted Access

Royal Netherlands Army
PO Box 90004
3509 AA Utrecht
Netherlands
+31 77 465 67 67

Press information:
+31 70 318 88 88
persvoorlichting@mindef.nl

Muscatatuck

39° 2′ 58.51″ N
85° 31′ 41.18″ W

Restricted Access

Muscatatuck Urban Training Center
+1 812-458-8780.
PO Box 77. Butlerville, IN 47223
Muscatatuck Public Affairs Office:
+1 317 247-3300, Ext. 41610

Renting scheduling:
+1 317 247 3300, Ext. 41777
ng.in.inarng.list.mutc-sched@mail.mil

Muscatatuck Urban Training Center,
4230 E Administration Drive, Butlerville, IN 47223, USA

Muscatatuck holds an open house day once a year (September–October). Games, demonstrations and tours allow the visitor to get familiar with the training facility. Information is usually posted through social media.

MUTC can be rented for training to federal and non-federal entities, including government agencies, military units, non-profit organisations, Department of Defence contractors and more.

Muscatatuck is served by Indianapolis International Airport and Louisville International Airport. They are both an hour and a half by car. From Indianapolis, take I-65 S towards Louisville. Take exit 68 for IN-46 E towards Columbus. Continue on IN-46E for 36 km and turn left onto US-50 E. After about 13 km, turn left again onto N425 until you reach your destination. If you are coming from Louisville, take I-65N until exit 50A to merge onto US-50E. After almost 50 km, turn left onto N425 to Muscatatuck. There is no public transport available.

Medina Wasl / Medina Jabal

US Army's National Training Centre,
Fort Irwin Rd, Fort Irwin, CA 92310, USA

The National Training Centre organises box tours. Requirements for the tour: let the PAO office know which location you will arrive at. Wear closed-toe shoes and bring eye protection. Individuals who are not wearing closed-toe shoes will not be allowed to board the bus. Please carry a government issued ID (military ID or driver's license for US citizens; passport for non-US citizens). Bring bottled water. Lunch will be a Military Meal Ready to Eat, or you may bring a bag lunch. The training area consists of rugged terrain and is not handicap accessible.

Medina Wasl's and Medina Jabal's nearest airports are located in Ontario, CA (194 km), Los Angeles, CA (280 km) and Las Vegas, NV (290 km). For both northerly and southerly directions take I 15 and get off at exit 189, onto Fort Irwin Rd. Drive approximately 60 km until you reach the front gate. There are no gas stations between Barstow and Fort Irwin, so make sure you have enough petrol before exiting on Fort Irwin Road. There are public buses operating between Burstow and Fort Irwin.

35° 20′ 58.07″ N
116° 35′ 39.10″ W (Wasl)

35° 19′ 50.55″ N
116° 31′ 16.52″ W (Jabal)

Restricted Access

Contact info:
usarmy.irwin.tc.mbx.ft-irwin-pao@army.mil

Visitor Information Center:
Open Monday-Friday/0600-1800
Questions regarding installation access please call: 760 380-4905/6750

Box tours registration:
https://home.army.mil/irwin/index.php/about/visitor-information/ntc-tours
or at Fort Irwin's social media channels

Wadi al-Sahara

34° 24′ 21.61″ N
116° 16′ 28.89″ W

Restricted Access

https://www.29palms.marines.mil/

Tour contact:
+1 760 830-3735

Marine Corps Air Ground Combat Centre Twentynine Palms,
901 Adobe Rd, Twentynine Palms, San Bernardino, CA 92277, USA

The Commanding General's Tours Program provides a unique opportunity for adults 18 and above to tour the Combat Centre. Check with tour contact for dates. There are no tours available in June, July and August. Visitors must be able to walk through deep sand and on rugged terrain. The tour lasts between six to eight hours. Water is provided.

Twentynine Palms is located 260 km from L.A. International Airport (a three-hour drive) and approximately 95 km from Palm Springs Airport. If you are getting there by car take I-10 East or West depending on your departure point until exit 117. Take the exit and get onto CA-62 towards Twentynine Palms / Yucca Valley. After about 65 km, turn left onto Adobe Rd and it will take you to the main gate for MCAGCC.

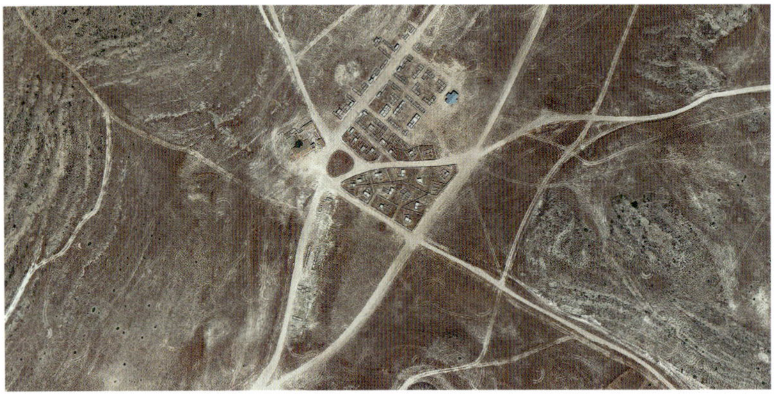

Chinchilla

Centro Nacional de Adiestramiento Chinchilla,
Paraje Rincón de Haro, s/n Chinchilla de Montearagón,
02520 Albacete, Spain

Chinchilla is a less than a three-hour drive from Madrid International Airport. Exit the Airport and get onto M-40. Take exit 13 to merge onto R-3 towards Valencia. After 30 km merge onto A-3. After 143 km keep right to continue on A-31. Then take exit 93 towards Horna, turn left at CM-3255 and then turn right. Continue for about 3 km and then turn left. Your destination will appear right after you pass Rincón de Haro. Albacete is the closest city to the installation. You can get onto A-31 from there and follow the former instructions.

38° 58′ 0.25″ N
1° 37′ 49.17″ W

No Access

Personnel office:
ofapet164@et.mde.es
+34 967198059

Anaconda

37° 57′ 8.26″ N
85° 48′ 54.22″ W

Restricted Access

https://home.army.mil/knox/index.php

Public Affairs Office:
usarmy.knox.id-training.mbx.pao@army.mil
+1 502 624-4985

US Army Fort Knox,
17 Bullion Blvd, Fort Knox, KY 40121, USA

Non-military organisations (e.g. civilian gun clubs or other civic organisations) desiring to utilise any portion of the training complex can submit a request to the Fort Knox PAO detailing the activities to be conducted and the facilities requested for use.

Louisville International Airport is the closest one to Fort Knox. Take I-65 South and take exit 125 to merge onto KY-841W. After 16 km take the exit towards US-31W. Follow 31W for approximately 30 minutes to the entrance gates of Fort Knox. If you are driving and coming from the South, take I-65 North to Elizabethtown, then take US-31W until Fort Knox exit. The main gate at Bullion entrance is open 24-hours.

KASOTC

King Abdullah II Special Operations Training Center,
2XGH+G6P, Yajouz Rd, Amman, Jordan

KASOTC is a closed to the public. You can only visit the site if you are willing to take one of their training courses, or if you are an active member of any military unit, agency or special forces group. If all fails, you can always opt to participate in the Annual Warrior Competition.

KASOTC is located about 20 km north from Amman city centre, Jordan's capital. From Queen Alia International Airport (AMM) it is just a one-hour drive. Take the Airport Rd / Route 15 / Route 45M. Follow Airport Rd and turn right to merge onto Amman Development Corridor / Route 45M after 12 km. Continue on Amman Development Corridor and the turn left onto Yajouz Rd / Route 30. After about 16 km your destination will appear to your right.

There is no public transport available from the city.

32° 1′ 53.06″ N
35° 58′ 31.12″ E

No Access

http://www.kasotc.com/

Warrior Competition:
http://warriorcompetition.com/

KASOTC contact:
info@kasotc.com
+962 6 560 9630

Jeoffrécourt / CTZUB

49° 32′ 45.02″ N
3° 58′ 2.83″ E (Jeoffrécourt)

49° 33′ 27.02″ N,
3° 55′ 1.95″ E (CTZUB)

Restricted Access
(Jeoffrécourt)

No Access
(CTZUB)

Contact information:
+33 4 62 88 91 84
CENZUB@icloud.com

Rue'Stick:
https://laruestick.adeorun.com/infos

Centre d'entraînement aux actions en zone urbaine (CENZUB),
15 Rue du 8 Mai 1945, 02150 Military Camp Sissonne, Aisne, France

You can visit Jeoffrécourt if you are fit and willing to participate in the Rue'Stick, the annual obstacle course organised by the CENZUB 94RI. You may choose between the Discovery course (7 km with obstacles at an affordable level) or the high-intensity course (8 km with obstacles for experienced athletes). Numerous activities are held during the race: catering, picnic areas, games for children (inflatable course, pony rides, laser shooting) as well as recruitment information.

The CENZUB is located within the Sissonne Military Camp. The closest international airport serving it is Paris Charles de Gaulle, which is just one hour and 40 minutes drive away. Exit the Airport on N 1102 and merge onto A2. When you get to Soissons keep left to stay on N2. After about 33 km, once you pass Laon, turn right and merge onto D1044, then turn left onto D181. When you get to Sissonne, cross the town – turning right onto Rue Saint-Martin, left onto Rue du Général de Gaulle and left again onto Rue de Roucy. After 500 m turn right onto Rue du 8 Mai 1945, until you reach your destination. It will appear in front of you.

The closest train station is at Saint Erme. There are regular trains from Reims. Saint Erme is just 7 km away.

Schnöggersburg

Gefechtsübungszentrum Heer, Salchauer Chaussee 1, Altmark-Kaserne, 39638 Gardelegen / OT Letzlingen, Saxony-Anhalt, Germany

Schnöggersburg is closed to the public. There is, however, an annual open day which features music, entertainment, horse-drawn carriages as well as a dynamic weapons display. The event is usually promoted on the German Army social media.

Schnöggersburg is served by Berlin Brandenburg Airport to the East and Flughafen Hannover-Langenhagen to the West. They are both less than a two-hour drive away.

From Berlin's Airport, get on A113 from Schönefelder Allee, after 5 km, at the interchange 10-Kreuz Schönefelder Kreuz, use the right two lanes to follow signs for A10 towards Magdeburg/Leipzig/Potsdam. Continue on A10 and the keep left to continue on A2 for about 95 km. At the interchange 68-Kreuz Magdeburg, use the right lane to follow signs for A14 towards Salzwedel/Haldensleben. Continue on B71 to your destination in Gardelegen. It will appear on the left. From Hannover, head south-east towards Flughafenstrasse. Continue onto B522. Take the exit towards A2. Keep left, follow signs for A2 and merge onto A2. Continue onto A2 for 92.7 km. Take the exit 65-Eilsleben towards B245. Then follow B245 and B71 to your destination in Gardelegen.

52° 29′ 16.43″ N,
11° 36′ 33.88″ E

Restricted Access

https://www.bundeswehr.de/en/contact

Schnöggersburg Press Office:
+49 39088 90-1010

IMAGE SOURCES

The vast majority of images used in this book are either screenshots from videos, military photographs classified as public domain and open license images. The appearance of visual information from the US Department of Defense, the UK Ministry of Defence, the French Ministère des Armées and the Ministerie van Defensie of the Netherlands does not imply or constitute their endorsement. Every effort has been made to contact the copyright holders of the other images used in this book. The publishing house and the author would like to extend their gratitude to all of those who have given permission for their work to be reproduced here.
The following is the list of the illustration sources.

Page 16 *from left to right:*

Author's screenshot, Canadian and American soldiers conduct an urban assault during ex allied spirit, Canadian Forces Combat Camera video, Crown Copyright, 2016.

Photo by Marco Smed, Afghanistan in der Oberpfalz, UniSPIEGEL 4, 2005.

Page 17:

Photo by Left4Dead, Report – STANTA Battle Area, Norfolk, www.28dayslater.co.uk. ,2011.

Page 19 *from left to right and top to bottom:*

Photo by Idavoll, Report Copehill Down FIBUA Site, www.28dayslater.co.uk, 2015.

Photo by Bob Wood,The Mock Village of Copehill Down, www.amunisngplanet.org, 2014.

Photo by Chris Talbot, Salisbury Plain- Copehill Training Village, www.geograph.org.uk, 2012.

Photo by Idavoll, Report Copehill Down FIBUA Site, www.28dayslater.co.uk, 2015.

Photo by Idavoll, Report Copehill Down FIBUA Site, www.28dayslater.co.uk, 2015.

Photo by Chris Talbot, Salisbury Plain- Copehill Training Village, www.geograph.org.uk, 2012.

Copehill Down village at Salisbury Plain provides our Armed Forces customers with the facilities they need to train effectively, Crown Copyright, MOD 2018.

Photo by Urbex Se, Copehill Down Salisbury Plain, www.derelictplaces.co.uk, 2017.

Page 21 *from left to right and top to bottom:*

Photo by Esko Townell, A view, looking north, of the center of the combat village at the Military Operations in Urban Terrain (MOUT) Collective Training Facility, The U.S. National Archives, 1990.

Combat town, MCB Camp Lejeune, 0311 Tactical Solutions LLC, 2011.

Military Builds Another Fake "American Looking" City for Urban Warfare Training, photo, www.truthandaction.org.

Photo by Esko Townell, A view, looking southwest from the church steeple, of the combat village at the Military Operations in Urban Terrain (MOUT) Collective Training Facility,The U.S. National Archives, 1990.

Photo by Esko Townell, A view of the city hall, left, and townhouses in the combat village at the Military Operations in Urban Terrain (MOUT) Collective Training Facility, The U.S. National Archives, 1990.

Photo by Esko Townell, A view of a church, right background, townhouses and a building with simulated artillery/bomb damage on the northern edge of the combat village at the Military Operations in Urban Terrain (MOUT) Collective Training Facility, The U.S. National Archives, 1990.

Author's screenshot, 2nd Battalion, 6th Marine Regiment FEX II, video by Lance Cpl. Samuel Taylor, U.S. Marine Corps 2016.

Author's screenshot, 2nd Battalion, 6th Marine Regiment FEX II, video by Lance Cpl. Samuel Taylor, U.S. Marine Corps 2016.

Page 23 *from left to right and top to bottom:*

Author's screenshot, Urban Close Air Support, video by Cpl Waiyan Tin, U.S. Marine Corps, 2015.

Photo by Lance Cpl. Danny Gonzalez, Urban Close Air Support Day & Night, U.S. Marine Corps, 2016.

Author's screenshot, Urban Close Air Support, video by Lance Cpl. Jeremy Laboy, U.S. Marine Corps, 2015.

Munitions Response & Range Services, Yodaville Target Area, Bering Sea group. Corporate newsletter, 2013.

Page 25 *from left to right and top to bottom:*

Author's screenshot, 'Spookdorp' voor militaire oefeningen. Achter Gesloten Deuren, video by NU.nl, 2019.

Photo by Catharina Gerritsen, A village without inhabitants, Knuckleheads blog, 2013.

Author's screenshot, 'Spookdorp' voor militaire oefeningen. Achter Gesloten Deuren, video by NU.nl, 2019.

Author's screenshot, 'Spookdorp' voor militaire oefeningen. Achter Gesloten Deuren, video by NU.nl, 2019.

Photo by Collectie Nederlands Instituut voor Militaire Historie, Het Korps Commandotroepen en buitenlandse eenheden tijdens de oefening Black Tulip in het oefendorp Marnehuizen in 2005, Defensiekrant 14, 2019.

Page 26:

Muscatatuck Urban Training Complex (MUTC) Subterranean Trainer, Tilt Up Concrete Association.

Page 27 *from left to right and top to bottom:*

Photo by TSgt Tony Tolley, A simulated flooded housing community can be seen at the Muscatatuck Urban Training Center at Camp Atterbury, Ind, United States Air Force, Department of Defense, 2012.

Photo by Pvt. Daniel Alkana, A train sits derailed as Soldiers participate in Vibrant Response 19 at Muscatatuck Urban Training Center, Indiana, U.S. Army, 2019.

Photo by Staff Sgt. Brad Staggs, Exercise Vibrant Response 12, U.S. Army, 2012.

Author's screenshot, Muscatatuck Hosts Annual Disaster Response Military Exercise, video, 2018.

Photo by Lance Cpl. Quinn Hurt, Marine Corps Warfighting Lab experiments with urban combat concepts, U.S. Marine Corps, 2019

Page 29 *from left to right and top to bottom:*

Photo by Rafael Ben Ari, General view of Tze'elim urban warfare center, 2011.

Photo by John Rice, USACE helps Israeli Air Force move to the Negev Desert, U.S. Army Corps of Engineer, 2009.

Unknown source.

Author's screenshot, War Games: Israeli Urban Warfare, video by Vice News, 2014.

Photo by Lance Cpl. Patrick Katz, 11th MEU Mala National Training Center in Israel, U.S. Marine Corps, 2021.

Page 30:

Photo by John F. Williams, U.S. Marines with 3rd Battalion, 1st Marine Regiment, engage virtual arab civilians, while improving their skills with the Infantry Immersion Trainer, U.S. Navy, U.S. Federal Government, 2008.

Page 31 *from left to right and top to bottom:*

Photo by Senior Airman Caleb Pierce, Allied Strike 10, U.S. Air Force, 2010.

Photo by Casey Bain, JMRC, joint and coalition partners prep IBCT for Afghanistan mission, U.S. Joint Forces, Department of Defence.

Combat Resolve X (85), Ministry of Defense of Ukraine, 2018.

Photo by Sgt. Christina Dion, Bulgarian land forces take on opposing forces of 1-4 Infantry, U.S. Army, 2014.

Combined Resolve X. How the Ukrainians surprised NATO, AverMAN. World creative news, 2018.

Photo by Sgt. Christina Dion, Sandhurst, West Point cadets perform village clearning maneuvers in joint exercise at Hohenfels Training Area, U.S. Army, 2014.

Photo by Fritz-Wolfgang Etzold / VNP, Klein-Afghanistan in Hohenfelds, Nordbayern, 2012.

Page 33 *from left to right and top to bottom:*

Author's screenshot, A look at the U.S. Army's artificial city of Ujen, video, 2017.

Unknown source

Author's screenshot, Fort Irwin "The Box" NTC National Training Center (USA), video by Global URBEX, 2014.

Author's screenshot, A look at the U.S. Army's artificial city of Ujen, video, 2017.

Author's screenshot, Fort Irwin "The Box" NTC National Training Center (USA), video by Global URBEX, 2014.

Photo by Sgt. Rodney Foliente, Combat medics practise their trade at NTC (Image 2 of 3), U.S. Army, 2008.

Photo by Peter Bohler, Soldiers hunt for insurgents during a scenario in the village. A cameraman films the action from the turret of the mosque for later analysis, 2009.

Page 34:

Photo by Peter Bohler, Muyuad, an Iraqi who role-plays the Iraqi Police Chief, in his room. He shares this shipping container with a roommate, 2009.

Page 35 *from left to right and top to bottom:*

Author's screenshot, Fort Irwin: A Desert Training Ground for U.S. Soldiers, video by Voice of America News, 2018.

Author's screenshot, Fort Irwin: A Desert Training Ground for U.S. Soldiers, video by Voice of America News, 2018.

Photo by Spc. Angel Heraldez, Holding the Line (2/18), U.S. Army, 2018.

Author's screenshot, Fort Irwin box tour, video by Sundevillion, YouTube channel, 2017.

Photo by Spc. Angel Heraldez, Holding the Line (1/18), U.S. Army, 2018.

Façades and Walls, Strategic Operations, Inc.

Author's screenshot, Fort Irwin: A Desert Training Ground for U.S. Soldiers, video by Voice of America News, 2018.

Photo by Brooks O. Hubbard IV, Corps sends team to Fort Irwin to assess monsoon damage, The U.S. Army Corps of Engineers, 2013.

Page 36:

Author's screenshot, Human terrain, video by David Udris, James Der Derian and Michael Udris, Udris Film, 2010.

Page 37 *from left to right and top to bottom:*

Author's screenshot, DCSC Marines Uphold 2nd Marine Division Standards, video by Cpl. Krista James, U.S. Marine Corps, 2015.

Photo by Lance Cpl. Chris Garcia House to house: 2/2 Golf, U.S. Marine Corps, 2015.

Author's screenshot, 2/2 Completes MOUT, video by Lance Cpl. Juan A. Soto-Delgado, U.S. Marine Corps, 2016.

Author's screenshot, 26th Marine Expeditionary Unit, Battalion Landing Team, 2nd Battalion, 6th Marine Regiment, Realistic Urban Training, video by Cpl. Adam D Edwards, U.S. Marine Corps, 2017.

Author's screenshot, 26th Marine Expeditionary Unit, Battalion Landing Team, 2nd Battalion, 6th Marine Regiment, Realistic Urban Training, video by Cpl. Adam D Edwards, U.S. Marine Corps, 2017.

Page 39 *from left to right and top to bottom:*

Photo by Allied Joint Force Command Brunssum, Air Assault Operation, Spanish SOF, Chinchilla, Trident Juncture 15, Combat Camera Team of LPAO Chinchilla TJ15, 2015.

Author's screenshot, Rural and Urban Operations enhance the capabilities of the NATO Response Force, Courtesy Video Natochannel, 2015.

Author's screenshot, FTX resumen ejercicio BRIMAR 2, video, 2022.

Author's screenshot, Rural and Urban Operations enhance the capabilities of the NATO Response Force, Courtesy Video Natochannel, 2015.

Page 41 *from left to right and top to bottom:*

Author's screenshot, 123rd STS Training, video by Master Sgt. Philip Speck, U.S. Air Force 2013.

Author's screenshot, 123rd STS Training, video by Master Sgt. Philip Speck, U.S. Air Force 2013.

Author's screenshot, Airsoft Urban Combat using Vholdr HD Helmetcam, video by Raymond, YouTube channel, 2010.

Author's screenshot, 123rd STS Training, video by Master Sgt. Philip Speck, U.S. Air Force 2013.

Photo by Master Sgt. Philip Speck, Kentucky Air Guard special tactics unit trains in "Afghan" village at Fort Knox, U.S. Air National Guard, 2013.

Author's screenshot, Airsoft Urban Combat using Vholdr HD Helmetcam, video by Raymond, YouTube channel, 2010.

Photo by Master Sgt. Philip Speck, Members of the Kentucky Air National Guard's 123rd Special Tactics Squadron clear a building during close-quarters combat training at Zussman Range, U.S. Air National Guard, 2013.

***Page 42** from left to right:*

Photo by Andy Cargill ABIPP, Opening of new Middle Eastern Training area at Stanta in Norfolk 2,UK MoD, Crown Copyright, 2009.

Photo by Andy Cargill ABIPP, Opening of new Middle Eastern Training area at Stanta in Norfolk 2, UK MoD, Crown Copyright, 2009.

***Page 43** from left to right and top to bottom:*

Author's screenshot, KASOTC 2013 with K9, video by Santiago Rod YouTube channel, 2013.

Courtesy photo, Foreign military sales (Image 2 of 2), U.S. Army Corps of Engineers, 2008.

Photo by KASOTC, Urban Area, KASOTC web page, 2009.

KASOTC Aircraft Trainer, www.strikehold.wordpress.com, 2009.

Author's screenshot, KASOTC 2013 with K9, video by Santiago Rod YouTube channel, 2013.

***Page 45** from left to right and top to bottom:*

Photo by Lance Cpl. Hailey Clay, ACMC Visits 29 Palms, U.S. Marine Corps, Communication Directorate, 2017.

Photo by Cpl. M. C. Nerl, Marines from 1st Battalion, 5th Marines, Camp Pendleton, Calif., take part in Enhanced Mojave Viper, a pre-deployment training exercise at the 274-acre Combined Arms Military Operations on Urban Terrain complex at Range 220, U.S. Marine Corps, 2011.

Photo by Staff Sgt. Carl Atherton, The Combat Center opens its newest, live fire, full immersion, Military Operations on Urban Terrain training range, U.S. Marine Corps, 2011.

Author's screenshot, Integrated Training Exercise (ITX) 1-17 Urban Exercise, video by Sgt. Patricia A. Morris, 2d MARDIV Combat Camera, U.S. Marine Corps, 2016.

Combined Arms M.O.U.T. Phase 1–3, Mosher Drew Architects.

***Page 45** from left to right:*

Photo by Lance Cpl. Tojyea G. Matally, BLT 2/6 Raids MOUT town during RUT, U.S. Marine Corps 2017.

Photo by Jared Brumbaugh, IED Training at Camp Lejeune, PRE Public Radio East, 2014.

***Page 47** from left to right:*

Déplacement du CEMA au Centre d'entraînement aux actions en zone urbaine – 94e régiment d'infanterie, Copyright Armée de Terre, 2018.

La 6 s'attaque au CTZUB!, 7e Bataillon de Chasseurs Alpins, Copyright Armée de Terre, 2017

Page 48:

Author's screenshot, Préparation opérationnelle avec le CENZUB, video by Armée de Terre, 2017.

***Page 49** from left to right and top to bottom:*

Untitled, Cenzub 94ème RI, Copyright Armée de Terre, 2017.

Photo by Guillaume Bela, Le Cenzub français, Forces Operations blog, 2013.

Author's screenshot, video by CENZUB 94RI, Copyright Armée de Terre, 2017.

Les explosions éclatent devant les anneaux olympiques, Copyright Armée de Terre, 2015.

Jeoffrécourt, Cenzub 94ème RI, Copyright Armée de Terre, 2017.

Author's screenshot, Le 92e RI combat en zone urbaine – Mars 2013, video by SIRPA Terre Image, Copyright Armée de Terre, 2013

Photo by G. Garitan Journée portes ouvertes, 2016.

Photo by Sgt. Kassie McDole, SPMAGTF-CR-AF Bravo Co & French Army Conduct Platoon Defense exercise, U.S. Marine Corps, 2017.

***Page 51** from left to right and top to bottom:*

Author's screenshot, VJTF2019 Schnelle Eingreiftruppe-Kampf um Schnöggersburg, video by Matthias Baumann, BTB-concept, 2018.

Author's screenshot, VJTF2019 Schnelle Eingreiftruppe-Kampf um Schnöggersburg, video by Matthias Baumann, BTB-concept, 2018.

Photo by Chris Wohlt, Bedrückend! – Meine Heimat als Kriegsgebiet, ct-press, 2017.

Photo by Björn Müller, The market place of Schnöggersburg old quarter, published at German armed forces open part of new training city for urban warfare, www.pivotarea.eu, 2017.

Photo by Duncan Campbell, Exercise IRON STORM 23, UK MOD, Crown copyright 2023.

Photo by Duncan Campbell, Exercise IRON STORM 23, UK MOD, Crown copyright 2023.

Author's screenshot, Schnöggersburg – Erster Durchgang mit Truppe – Bundeswehr, video by Bundeswehr, 2018.

Author's screenshot, Schnöggersburg – Erster Durchgang mit Truppe – Bundeswehr, video by Bundeswehr, 2018.

***Page 52** from left to right:*

Author's screenshot, Fuseliers in oefendorp Schnöggersburg, video by 13 Lichte Brigade, Ministerie van Defensie, 2018.

Author's screenshot, Fuseliers in oefendorp Schnöggersburg, video by 13 Lichte Brigade, Ministerie van Defensie, 2018.

***Page 56:** from left to right:*

Author's screenshot, Short drone fight over Copehill Down on Salisbury Plain, video by Tom Palmer, YouTube channel, 2018.

Author's screenshot, Twee eenheden van onze brigade trainden tezamen in Marnehuizen, video by 43 Gemechaniseerde Brigade, Ministerie van Defensie, 2019

***Page 57** from left to right:*

Author's screenshot, War Games: Israeli Urban Warfare, video by Vice News, 2014.

Photo by Pfc. Kyle Edwards, Fort Irwin box tour, Fort Irwin Operations Group, U.S. Army, 2015.

Page 59:

Author's screenshot, Fire range 3, Google earth, 2005.

***Page 60** from left to right:*

Photo by Cpl. Medina Ayala-Lo, Combat Center conducts desert tortoise translocation (Image 7 of 27), U.S. Marine Corps, 2017.

Photo by Kelly O'Sullivan Desert Tortoise Headstart, U.S. Marine Corps, 2015.

***Page 61** from left to right:*

Aufspielen unter dem Regenbogen – wider den Krieg, Keine Wiedervereinigung mit dem Krieg, www.lebenslaute.net, 2018.

Photo by Paul Böhm, Nach 77 Jahren wieder Kirwa in Enslwang, www.mittelbayerische.de, 2015.

***Page 63** from left to right and top to bottom:*

Author's screenshot, War Games: Israeli Urban Warfare, video by Vice News, 2014.

Photo by Lance Cpl. Justin Bowles, Urban Leaders Course: The Experts in Urban Warfare, U.S. Marine Corps, 2016.

Photo by Cpl. Sonia Rodriguez,The Basic School (TBS), clears a window during urban operations training at Marine Corps Base Quantico, U.S. Marine Corps, 2014.

Photo by Lance Cpl. Garrett White, Kicking down doors (Image 2 of 10), U.S. Marine Corps, 2014.

Author's screenshot, 2nd Battalion, 6th Marine Regiment FEX II, video by Lance Cpl. Samuel Taylor, U.S. Marine Corps, 2016.

Photo by Emanuel Licha, The mock Iraqi/Afghan village is built from shipping containers, and its aspect is enhanced by set designers who come from the Hollywood film industry, film still Mirages, 2010.

Author's screenshot, Kiwis hone urban combat tactics in IIT, video by LCpl. David Staten, U.S. Marine Corps, 2015.

Photo by Cpl. Sonia Rodriguez, Alpha Company Conducts Urban Ops (Image 27 of 28), U.S. Marine Corps, 2014.

***Page 64** from left to right:*

Photo by Pfc. Eric T. Keenan, Marine Corps Warfighting Lab experiment may lead to possible change in target engagement (Image 4 of 6), U.S. Marine Corps, 2013.

Photo by Seth Robson, Soldiers employ live fire in mock raid at Hohenfels, © Stars and Stripes All Rights Reserved, 2006.

***Page 65** from left to right:*

Unknown source

Photo by Lance Cpl. Chris Garcia, CLB 1 conducts MOUT Training, U.S. Marine Corps, 2015.

Page 66:

Photo by Staff Sgt. Armando R. Limon, Combat Engineers test skills during stress shoot (Image 10 of 11), U.S. Army, 2017.

***Page 67** from left to right and top to bottom:*

Photo by Don Branum, Cadet 3rd Class Jared Hafich carries a mannequin representing an injured pilot toward a safehouse as other cadets in his fire team provide cover during a training exercise in Jacks Valley's mobile operations in urban terrain training area, U.S. Air Force, 2011.

Photo by Lindsey Leger, The Jordan team participates in the Airbus seizure event, demonstrating how to execute a target onboard a passenger aircraft, Little wars, 2015.

Hostage Rescue training scenarios are performed in the A300/B777 aircraft which is equipped with reactive threat targets and has nine entry points, the aircraft is also equipped with fourteen cameras and microphones to record the training, KASOTC, 2016.

Photo by Master Sgt. Michel Sauret, U.S. Army trains to respond to nuclear catastrophe, U.S. Army Reserve, 2017.

Photo by Spc. Jonathan Over, 222nd Broadcast Operations Detachment, Checking Inventory (Image 3 of 5), U.S. Army Reserve, 2017.

***Page 68** from left to right:*

Photo by Lance Cpl. Chris Garcia, CLB 1 conducts MOUT Training as part of LSE-15 (Image 1 of 5), U.S.Marines Corps, 2015.

Dorfleben, SST (Supply & Service Team) GmbH, 2014.

***Page 69** from left to right:*

Author's screenshot, Refugees Teach Cultural Awarness to Marines, video by Tech. Sgt. Wendy Day, U.S. Air Force, 2016.

Photo by Cpl. Peter R. Miller, A Marine with Battalion Landing Team, 3rd Battalion, 8th Marine Regiment, 22nd Marine Expeditionary Unit, motions for an Iraqi role-player to stay away during urban training at the Military Operations in Urban Terrain facility aboard Fort Pickett, Official Marine Corps, 2007.

Page 70:

Dorfleben, SST (Supply & Service Team) GmbH, 2014.

***Page 71** from left to right and top to bottom:*

Photo by Staff Sgt. Randy Florendo, Military Adviser Team – Police Adviser Team training exercise, U.S. Army, 2014.

Author's screenshot,13th MEU Maritime Raid Force Trains at Fort Irwin, video by Sgt. Christopher O'Quin, U.S. Marine corps, 2013.

Photo by Spc. Justin De Hoyos,Georgian mission rehearsal exercise (Image 1 of 3), U.S. Army, 2014.

Photo by Lance Cpl. Victor Barrera Camp Lejeune opens first East Coast Infantry Immersion Trainer (Image 3 of 3), U.S. Marine Corps, 2011.

Author's screenshot, Human terrain, video by David Udris, James Der Derian and Michael Udris, Udris Film, 2010.

Page 72:

Author's screenshot, 3/3 Urban Attack Training, video by Cpl. Danielle Rodrigues, I Marine Expeditionary Force, U.S. Marine Corps, 2016.

Page 73:

Photo by Lance Cpl. Ashlee Conove, Marines with 3/4 conduct Range 205 (Image 4 of 5), U.S. Marine Corps, 2018.

Page 74:

Photo by Sgt. John Baker, Autonomous Robotic Human Type Targets make their way off of a firing range at Camp Pendleton, U.S. Marine Corps, 2016.

***Page 75** from left to right and top to bottom:*

Author's screenshot, Marathon Targets Broll at Range 410A, video by Lance Cpl. Ashlee Conover and Lance Cpl. Jennessa Davey, U.S. Marine Corps 2018.

Author's screenshot, Marathon Targets Broll at Range 410A, video by Lance Cpl. Ashlee Conover and Lance Cpl. Jennessa Davey, U.S. Marine Corps 2018.

Marathon Targets most impressive display at Ft Benning Maneuver Conference, Marathon Targets, 2016.

Robot Targets May Be Solution to Improving Army Marksmanship, Marathon Targets, 2016.

Photo by Patrick A. Albright, MCoE PAO, A Robotic Human Type Target Demonstration is conducted by the Sniper Course, April 29, 2014 at Burroughs Range, U.S. Army 2014.

Robotic Human Type Target Demonstration is conducted by the Sniper Course, April 29, 2014 at Burroughs Range, U.S. Army Maneuver Center of Excellence, 2014.

Unknown source.

Marathon Targets, 2011.

***Page 77** from left to right:*

Army Reservists from 100 Field Squadron of The Royal Monmouthshire Royal Engineers (Militia), spent a busy weekend exercise at Copehill Down FIBUA (Fighting In Built Up Area) Village on Salisbury Plain, The Royal Monmouthshire Royal Engineers (Militia), MOD Crown Copyright, 2017.

Page 78/79:

Author's screenshot, 3/3 Urban Assault at ITX 2-16, video by Sgt. Donald Holbert, U.S. Marine Corps, 2016.

Page 80:

Photo by Matt Masin, Camp Pendleton training includes actors, a fake village and simulated warfare, Southern California News Group, 2016.

***Page 81** from left to right:*

Photo by Donald Teft CIV, A view of the U.S. Army Stabilization Force (SFOR) Military Operations in Urban Terrain (MOUT) collective training facility at Fort Stewart, GA, The U.S. National Archives, 2000.

Photo by Kevin C Mcdevitt, Range 59E 403d Civil Affairs Battalion Conducted Explosive Hazard Awareness, Convoy Operations 09–10 Jan 2023 (Image 3 of 4), U.S. ASA Fort Dix Training Support Center / Dan Amburg, 2023

***Page 82** from left to right and top to bottom:*

Photo by Elaine Wilson, A recently built mosque at the Muscatatuck Urban Training Center, United States Department of Defense, 2011.

Photo by Jarek Tuszyński, "Mosque" at Medina Wasl, a mock Iraqi village used to train troops in urban warfare, 2011.

Asymmetric Warfare Group Training Complex, W.M. Jordan Company.

Combined Arms Collective Training Facility (CACTF) Ft. Hood, Emerson Construction, Inc.

Mosque, catalogue image Allied Container Systems, 2010.

Photo by Scott T. Sturkol, Fort McCoy's Combined Arms Collective Training Facility (Image 25 of 29), U.S. Army, 2018.

MOUT Range Structures and Storage Units, UNICOR catalogue, Federal Prison Industries program, 2012.

Another religious center (Mosque) populates a training area, Strategic Operations, Inc.

***Page 83** from left to right and top to bottom:*

Mosques and Statues, Strategic Operations, Inc.

Mosque, Strategic Operations, Inc.

Author's screenshot, Fort Irwin: A Desert Training Ground for U.S. Soldiers, video by VOA News (Voice of America), 2018.

Author's screenshot, Fort Irwin: A Desert Training Ground for U.S. Soldiers, video by VOA News (Voice of America), 2018.

Photo by Master Sgt. Mark Burrell, 352nd CACOM, "On Purpose; With a Purpose" Army Civil Affairs Troops Triumph at NTC Training (Image 13 of 18), U.S. Army, 2016.

MOUT Buildings, Western Metal Supply Co. Inc. Product brochure, 2018.

Military Training Temple case strudy. MOUT training village for U.S. Air Force IED training, Falcon Structures, 2010.

Mosque, Allied Container Systems catalogue, 2010

***Page 85** from left to right and top to bottom:*

Photo by Aaron Vanek, Larp at the National Training Center at Fort Irwin, 2011. Used with permission.

Photo by Matt Masin, Prop kebabs and a sheep provide some realism during Pacific Rim exercises at Camp Pendleton, Southern California News Group, 2016.

Author's screenshot, Fort Irwin "The Box" NTC National Training Center (USA), video by Global Urbex YouTube channel, 2014.

MOUT training areas force troops to dismount and interact with the population, Strategic Operations, Inc.

Author's screenshot, Fort Irwin "The Box" NTC National Training Center (USA), video by Global Urbex YouTube channel, 2014.

Page 86:

Author's screenshot, Canadian Army vs Albanian Army – Canadian Army Training to Defend Village from Albanian Attack, video by Markus Rauchenberger, Training Support Activity Europe, U.S. Army 2014

Page 87:

Author's screenshot, MIX-16 B-Roll, video by Lance Cpl. Molly Hampton, U.S. Marine Corps, 2016.

Page 89:

Unknown source.

Page 91:

Author's screenshot, Muscatatuck Unveiled Episode 01, video by Spc. David Bonnell and Sgt. Brad Staggs, U.S. Army, 2010.

Page 92:

Munitions Response & Range Services, Bering Sea Group, Corporate newsletter, 2013.

***Page 93** from left to right and top to bottom:*

Photo by Cpl. M. C. Nerl, Marines from 1st Battalion, 5th Marines, Camp Pendleton, Calif., take part in Enhanced Mojave Viper, a pre-deployment training exercise at Range 220, U.S. Marine Corps, 2011.

Photo by Cpl. Jeremiah Handeland, Marines in an exercise at Range 220, U.S. Marine Corps, 2011.

Author's screenshot, U.S. and Mexican Marines Conduct Integrated Infantry Immersion Training, Pendleton, video by Cpl. Desiree D King, U.S. Marine Corps, 2018.

Author's screenshot, Marine Corps Warfighting Lab experiments with urban combat concepts, video by Lance Cpl. Quinn Hurt, U.S. Marine Corps, 2019.

Author's screenshot, Integrated Training Exercise (ITX) 1-17 Urban Exercise, video by Sgt. Patricia A. Morris, 2d MARDIV Combat Camera, U.S. Marine Corps, 2016.

***Page 97** from left to right:*

Photo by Collectie Nederlands Instituut voor Militaire Historie, Het Korps Commandotroepen en buitenlandse eenheden tijdens de oefening Black Tulip in het oefendorp Marnehuizen in 2005, Defensiekrant 14, 2019.

Photo by David Altrath, Destroyed building, The Ghost Town Series, 2020.

***Page 96** from left to right:*

Military Operations on Urban Terrain Collective Training Facility (MOUT) Camp Shelby, JBHM Architecture, www.jbhm.com, 2007.

Photo by Ron Glaze, Impossible City, Fort Ord, www.fortord.net, 2006.

***Page 99** from left to right:*

Photo by Esko Townell, A view of a structure with simulated artillery/bomb damage in the combat village at the Military Operations in Urban Terrain (MOUT) Collective Training Facility, The U.S. National Archives, 1990.

Author's screenshot, Several public safety agencies meet at the Guardian Training Center in Perry for disaster training, video by Matt Thielke (WGXA), 2017.

***Page 102** from left to right:*

Infrastructure de tirs en zone urbaine – Sissonne, Demathieu Bard, 2010.

FASTC Explosive Sim Alley, State Department, 2019.

***Page 103** from left to right:*

Photo by Lance Cpl. Sahara Luna, 1st Tanks Glass House drills, U.S. Marine Corps,2019.

Unknown source

***Page 104** from left to right:*

Delta MOUT, TwentyNine Palms, CA, Training Facilities & Ranges, Amidon Ballistic Concrete Inc., 2018.

Shooting Ranges, Ballenger International, LLC

***Page 107** from left to right:*

Photo by Michael Thormann, Trainings-Gebäude, das bei Combined Resolve VII als Elektronikladen dient, www.mithor.de, 2017.

Photo by Corporal Rob Kane, British Army Expo 22, UK MOD, Crown Copyright 2022.

***Page 108** from left to right:*

Photo by Catharina Gerritsen, A village without inhabitants, Knuckleheads blog, 2013.

Author's screenshot, California Army National Guard Infantry Soldiers Conduct Urban Assault Training B-Roll Package, video by Staff Sgt. Yvonne Najera, U.S. Army, 2014.

***Page 109** from left to right:*

7th Special Forces Group Range Complex, Benham Engineering Company.

Photo by Tech. Sgt. Ted Nichols, Lithuanian partners visit Fort Indiantown Gap training facilities, U.S. Air National Guard, 2016.

***Page 112** from left to right:*

Author's screenshot, Royal Marines 40 Commando | Urban training in Indiana, video by The Royal Marine, Crown Copyright, 2019.

Two Urban Sniper Hides, Tier 1 Group, LLC, 2017.

***Page 113** from left to right:*

Two Urban Sniper Hides, interior, Tier 1 Group, LLC, 2017.

Revolutionary Façade Technology System Photo-Immersive Realistic Aides for Training Environments (P.I.R.A.T.E.™), Military Wraps Defense System, 2013.

***Page 116** from left to right:*

Author's screenshot, Wintermarsch durch den Übungsplatz Hohenfels, 2020.

Photo by Bdr Murray Kerr, Exercise Dynamic Victory 2020 UK MOD, Crown Copyright 2020.

***Page 120** from left to right:*

This is Our Army – Fort Irwin, California, U.S. Army, 2007.

Photo by Nakaryak, The world's largest training ground for street-fighting tactics. Israel, www.livejournal.com, 2015.

***Page 121** from left to right:*

Photo published Bundeswehr IUD Twitter, 2023.

NTC Opening New Urban Training Site, U.S. Army, 2007.

***Page 122** from left to right:*

Fort Benning site. The MARS (Mobile Autonomous Robot Software) research project, The Mobile Robot Laboratory, College of Computing, Georgia Institute of Technology, 2020.

MOTC-MOUT Defined, BANAIR Range Equipment Brochure, 2020.

***Page 124** from left to right:*

The Combined Arms Collective Training Facility (CACTF), Fort Indiantown Gap, National Guard., U.S. Department of Defense.

Author's screenshot, Highlighting Camp Shelby Joint Forces Training Center, video by Lt. Col. Deidre Smith, U.S. Army, 2015.

Page 125:

Unknown source.

Page 126:

Google Earth Image, 2021.

***Page 127** from left to right:*

SAFTI City's Phase 1 will be completed next year, consisting of 60 new training buildings, and roads that can be reconfigured to different layouts for our soldiers to train in complex urban environments, photo published Ng Eng Hen Twitter post, 2023.

Author's screenshot, The conclusion of the joint military exercise "Cooperation 3" between the UAE and the Sultanate of Oman, video by WAM. 2023.

Pages 129 to 144:

Various Sites, Google Earth Images, 2022.

BIBLIOGRAPHY

Books:

Stephen Graham, Cities Under Siege: The New Military Urbanism, Verso, 2010.

Ersela Kripa and Stephen Mueller, Fronts, Applied Research and Design Publishing, 2020.

Derek Gregory, The Colonial Present, Blackwell, 2004.

Tom Vanderbilt, Survival City, University of Chicago Press, 2010.

Corey Mead, War Play: Video Games and the future of armed conflict, Eamon Dolan Books, 2013.

James Der Derian, Virtuous War, Routledge, 2001.

Jean Baudrillard, Simulations, Semiotext, 1983.

Adam Broomberg and Oliver Chanarin, Chicago: Everything that Happened, Happened Here First, Steidl.

Russell W. Glen, Combat in Hell, Rand (National Defense Research Institute), 1996.

Military Manuals:

Urban Operations in the Year 2020, RTO technical report 71, NATO, 2003.

Introduction to Urban Operations 1, USA Marine Corps Basic Officer Course B4R5359.

Introduction to Urban Operations 2, USA Marine Corps Basic Officer Course B4R5379.

Combined Arms Operations in Urban Terrain, Field Manual, Department of the Army, FM3-06.11.

Military Operations on Urbanised Terrain (MOUT) Manual, U.S. Marine Corps MCRP 12-10B.1, 2016.

Intelligence support to urban operations, headquarters, Department of the Army, December 2015.

Reimagining the character of urban operations, Rand Corporation (National Defense Research Institute), 2007.

Preparing for the proven inevitable, Rand Corporation (National Defense Research Institute), 2006.

Urban Warfare Project, special series, Modern Warfare Institute.

Papers and articles:

Andrew Mack, The Politics of Asymmetric Conflict, World Politics, January 1975.

Andrea Kretschmann, "Krieg und artifizieller Städtebau", Wissenschaft und Frieden, February 2016..

Alix Valenti, MOUT Doctrine: Fighting in the Canyons, Armada International, 13.02.2017.

Alix Valenti, Preparing for battle, Armada International, 19.09.2017.

John Spencer, The Army Needs an Urban Warfare School, Modern War Institute, April 5, 2017.

Ian Dowdy, Evaluating Encroachment Pressures on the Military Mission, Sonoran Institute, 08.06.2017.

Adele Wilson, Military Terminology and the English Language, 2008.

Matti Friedman, The Peculiar Language of Soldiers, The Atlantic, 04.05.2016.

Luke Tress, When a dummy screams for help, Times of Israel, 25.08.2016.

Scott Magelssen, Theatre immersion and the simulation of theatres of war, Rehearsing the warrior ethics, March 2009.

Dabareh Vowell, Military Role Player Effectiveness, New Mexico Tech, August 2011.

Vince Beiser, Baghdad USA, Wired, June 2006.

Susan Schnuppli, "Improvised Explosive Designs", Borderlands, 2010.

Moving Targets will improve Marine skills, IITSEC, 28.11.2018.

Ted Thornhill, Wheeled target robots delivered to U.S. Army, Daily Mail, 03.12.2011.

Sean O'Hagan, Caught in the crosshairs, the Guardian art and design, 18.06.2014.

Vicente Javier Clemente-Suárez, Psycho-physiological response of soldiers in urban combat, Anales de Psicología, May 2013.

Mayor General Robert H. Scales, Urban Warfare: a soldier's view, Military Review, January 2005.

Stephen Graham, Postmortem City: Towards and urban geopolitics, City Journal Issue 2, 2004.

Dan Archibald, Adam Smith, Sunny Adams and Manroop Chawla, Military Training Lands Historic Context, U.S. Army Corps of Engineers, March 2010.

Davis, Assault on German Village, Der Spiegel, 11.10.1999.

Jonathan Glancey, Good bye to Berlin, The Guardian, 2003.

Rachel Woodward, Military Geography, The International Encyclopedia of Geography, 2017.

The Military-Pastoral Complex: Contemporary Representations of Militarism in the Landscape, Tate, 06.02.2018.

Ruth Dusseault, The Incomplete Illusion: Photographing the Training Ground, University of California Press, September 2013.

Roberto J. Gonzáles, The rise and fall of the human terrain system, Counterpunch, 29.07.2015.

Todd South, The future battlefield: Army, Marines prepare for 'massive' fight in megacities, Military Times, 01.07.2019.

Eyal Weizman, Walking through walls, Frontier Architectures, Steidl, 2007.

Phillip Misselwitz and Eyal Weizmann, Military Operations as Urban Planning, Mute, 28.08.2003.

John Spencer, Crossing the street, addressing one of urban warfare's greatest challenges, Modern War Institute, 30.10.2018.

Bryan Finoki, MOUT urbanism, Subtopia, 02.06.2018.

Specific to:

Baladia:

David Betz, Peering into the past and future of urban warfare in Israel, War on the rocks, 17.12.2015.

Barbara Opall-Rome, Marines to train at new Israeli combat center, Marine Corps Times, 25.06.2007.

Major General Nitsan Alon, Operational challenges, Vanderbilt journal for transnational law, 2018.

Preparing for more urban warfare, the Economist, special report, 25.01.2018.

Ad Van Denderen, Baladia city, VU l'agence, 2012.

Chinchilla:

Josechu Guillamón, 550 militares se forman en el Cenad, La Tribuna de Ciudad Real, 14.10.2018.

S. Jiménez, Cospedal se gasta 420,000 euros en simular un barrio árabe, Periodico CLM, 31.07.2017.

Centros de adiestramiento, Revista Ejercito, Noviembre 2007.

Eastmere:

Andrew Levy, Good morning Afghanistan, Daily Mail, 01.05.2009.

Julian Gavaghan, The mean 'Helmand' streets, Daily Mail, 24.01.2011.

Troops train in the Middle East of England, Government UK, 18.01.2011.

Hohenfels:

Kate Connoly, No lederhosen, we're Afghans, The Guardian, 08.04.2007.

Marco Smedt, Afghanistan in der Oberpfalz, Unispiegel, April 2005.

Paul Böhm, Nach 77 Jahren wieder Kirwa, Schmidmühlen Mittelbayrische, 26.11.2019.

Civilians on the battlefield, German Foreign Policy.com, 27.11.2018.

Michael Thormann, NATO probt Krieg in Deutschland, RT Deutschland, 27.01.2018.

Firma sucht Statisten für Nato-Kriegsübung, Berliner Morgenpost, 27.04.2018.

15 Tage auf dem Schlachtfeld, TAZ, 26.11.2019.

Die Geschichte, Markt-Hohenfels.de/6760-Geschichte.html.

Hohenfels Training Area, GlobalSecurity.org, 23.04.2018.

Jeoffrécourt / CTZUB:

Fantassins, Le Magazine D'information de L'infanterie, January 2012.

Travis Hensley, Laser Beams and Avatars, John W. Kluge Centre, Library of Congress, 28.03.2016.

Dans la ville fantôme de Jeoffrécourt les armées étrangères simulant la guerre, Le Point, 08.05.2016.

Juliette Demey, When the army plays war, Gratiane de Moustier, 22.01.2019.

KASOTC:

Josh Eells, Sleep-away camp for postmodern cowboys, NY Times, 19.07.2013.

Scott Packard, Defense Journal: Kings of a special ops playground, Gear Patrol, 12.12.2013.

Benjamin Schuetze, Privatising anti-terror training, Al Jazeera, 17.07.2017.

Marnehuizen:

Catherina Gerritsen, A village without inhabitants, Knuckleheads, 20.11.2013.

Elmar Keetman, Urban bulldog, Military machines international, August 2011.

Wiegertje Postma, Ateke Willemse, Stammenoorlog in Marnehuizen, Vice, 22.08.2011.

Medina Jabal / Medina Wasl:

Wells Tower, Under the god gun, Harper's Magazine, 2006.

Claire Beckett, Simulating Iraq, Fraction Magazine, 15.02.2018.

Derek Gregory, Sim Cities and theatres of war, geographical imaginations, 19.05.2013.

Geoff Manaugh, In The Box: A Tour Through the Simulated Battlefields of the U.S. National Training Center, www.bldgblog.com/2013/05/in-the-box-a-tour-through-the-simulated-battlefields-of-the-u-s-national-training-center/, last visit: 30.01.2024.

Anna Merlan, It takes a fake military village, Topic, 28.02.2019.

Alan Taylor, A replica of Afghanistan in the Mojave, The Atlantic, 18.09.2013.

Emanuel Licha, Mirages: an optical machine in the desert, Philosophy and Photography vol. 2 no. 1, 01.09.2011.

D. Filkins and J. Burns, Mock Iraqi villages in Mojave prepare troops for battle, NY Times, 01.05.2006.

Joe Donnelly, The tortoise and the tank face off at Fort Irwin, LA Weekly, 20.08.2008.

Daniel J. Calder, Iraqi village on Irwin, United States Army, 31.03.2008.

Dennis Steele, Between Hollywood and Hell, United States Army, July 2008.

Jon Michael Connor, LRC-Irwin keeps NTC ready, United States Army, 08.02.2017.

Major Jon Brierton, Operation sandcastle, Bulletin of Army Engineers, 2008.

FORSCOM Regulation 350-50-1, Training at the National Training Center, 29.10.2018.

Michelle Tan, Combat training rotations will increase to 18 days, Army Times, 06.02.2015.

Charlie Sherpa, Walking the TOC, Red Bull Rising blog, last visit: 08.11.2020.

Charlie Sherpa, Life on the FOB, Red Bull Rising blog, last visit: 09.11.2020.

Schnöggersburg:

CTC. Walter F. Ullrich, The German Army and urban operations, Military Simulation & Training Magazine, 21.01.2019.

Steve Przybilla, Eine Stadt für den Kriegsfall, Neue Zürcher Zeitung, 21.11.2017.

Edda Fahrenhorst, Schnöggersburg, https://blog.superlative-made-in-germany.de/schnoeggersburg-die-groesste-uebungsstadt-europas-beim-gefechtsuebungszentrum-heer/, last visit: 30.01.2024.

Schnöggersburg – Übungsstadt für die Bundeswehr, Ruhrkultour, 24.01.2019.

Wadi al-Sahara:

Jena Lee, Drawing 29 Palms, Incendiary Traces, 12.03.2013.

Richard Wheeler, Military performance and embodied knowledge, Incendiary Traces, 12.06.2015.

Julie Watson, $170 million mock city rises at Marine base, NBC News, 28.01.2011.

Malcolm Pirnie, Range environmental vulnerability assessment, 29 Palms, November 2008.

Mark Muckenfuss, Marines train in mock Iraqi village, Leatherneck, 27.12.2008.

Darrell R. Santschi, Marines unveil city-size urban warfare training at Twentynine Palms, The Press-Enterprise, 27.01.2011.

Tyler Stallings, Secession in the Desert, ARID, 18.06.2012.

Yodaville:

James W. Crawley, Bombs Away at Yodaville, San Diego Union-Tribune, 18.07.1999.

SWTTR Users' Guide, Naval Surface Warfare Center, August 2015.

Graham Smith, Target Yodaville, Daily Mail, 09.07.2012.

Ed Darack, Welcome to Yodaville, Air & Space Magazine, 26.03.2009.

Søren Augustesen, Training the trainer, Scandinavian Aviation Magazine, 06.02.2018.

Yuma Range SOP, StaO3710.6J, U.S. Marine Corps, 25.01.2013.

ACKNOWLEDGEMENTS

It has been a long journey full of surprising encounters, unsuspected acquaintances and rewarding discussions. I have received long-term encouragement from many friends and colleagues. My sincere thanks to Bruno Bakalović, who has designed the layout and the structure of the book and guided the visual composition from the earliest stages through to the final product; to Renee Tobe, who helped shape the content with her critical editing and tireless support; to Eugenia Troncoso, for her dedicated drafting skills, her implacable research and image sourcing capacity; and to Javier Ventosa for his enthusiasm and encouragement.

IMPRINT

An imprint of Walter de Gruyter GmbH, Berlin/Boston

Project management jovis: Charlotte Blumenthal
Production: Susanne Rösler
Copy editing and proofreading: Cecilia Tricker-Walsh
Drawings: Eugenia Troncoso
Cover: Bruno Bakalović, with a video still from 3/3 Urban Assault at ITX 2-1
Design and setting: Bruno Bakalović, Johanna Mendau (PLEXGROUP)
Lithography: PLEXGROUP
Printed in the European Union

Bibliographic information published by the Deutsche Nationalbibliothek. The Deutsche Nationalbibliothek lists this publication in the Deutsche Nationalbibliografie; detailed bibliographic data are available on the Internet at http://dnb.d-nb.de

jovis Verlag
Genthiner Straße 13
10785 Berlin

www.jovis.de

jovis books are available worldwide in select bookstores. Please contact your nearest bookseller or visit www.jovis.de for information concerning your local distribution.

ISBN 978-3-98612-098-6